D1100373

THEATRE OF DECONSTRUCTION
KAITAISHA [1991-2001]

劇団解体社 [1991-2001]

THEATRE OF DECONSTRUCTION
KAITAISHA [1991-2001]

劇団解体社 [1991-2001]

THEATRE OF DECONSTRUCTION
KAITAISHA [1991-2001]

劇団解体社 [1991-2001]

Photographs —————————— Miyauchi Katsu ／宮内勝
Design ———————————— Takagi Yoshihiko (bon graphics)／高木善彦（ボン・グラフィクス）
Cover Design ————————— STUDIO TERRY "overground"
Translator ————————————— Maeshiba Naoko (Dialogue part I)／前芝尚子（対話 第一部）
                           Masuda Koji (Dialogue part II)／増田康次（対話 第二部）
                           Adam Broinowski (Dialogue part I+II)／アダム・ブロノフスキ（対話 第一部＋第二部）
                           Kuwabara Ayako (Performance Biography)／桑原綾子（上演データ）
Editor ——————————————— Gekidan KAITAISHA ／劇団解体社
Associate Editor ——————— Fujita Yuki ／藤田雄己
                           Saito Miyuki ／齋藤みゆき
Special Thanks to ———————— Onuki Takashi ／大貫隆史
                           James Tyson ／ジェイムズ・タイソン
Supported by ———————————— The Saison Foundation ／財団法人セゾン文化財団

The Date of Publication ／発行日 —— September 1, 2001 ／ 2001 年 9 月 1 日　初版第 1 刷発行
Publisher ／発行者 ————————— Shimizu Shinjin ／清水信臣
Published by ／発行所———————— Gekidan KAITAISHA ／劇団解体社
                           Igarashi Bld.1F, 2-4-8, Yushima, Bunkyo-ku, Tokyo, Japan
                           〒 113-0034 東京都文京区湯島 2-4-8 五十嵐ビル 1F
                           Phone/Fax:+81-3-5802-5387
                           http://www.kaitaisha.com
                           gekidan@kaitaisha.com
Printer ／印刷所 ——————————— Shuho Bijutsu ／集峰美術

©2001 Gekidan KAITAISHA
Printed in Japan
Distribution in UK by Chapter, Cardiff.

ISBN4-9900991-0-9 C0074 ¥1500E
定価 1500 円＋税 ／ US$12 ／ DM25 ／ £8

Contents
目次

2

Gekidan KAITAISHA
PROFILE

Gekidan KAITAISHA, a maverick company of the Tokyo independent theatre scene, has been creating performances, merging a variety of theatrical styles, for more than 15 years.

Recently, KAITAISHA has been focusing on contemporary movement, absurd text and raw, emotional performance. Although the plays are constructed as theatre works, the content is narrated by physical movement and expression, not by language. Elements of Japanese Noh theatre and of contemporary dance are incorporated – for instance by Tatsumi Hijikata, the founder of Japanese Butoh dance, and by choreographers Pina Bausch and Martha Graham.

The performers are often bruised, by falling with no concern for gravity, or by turning themselves into percussive instruments. Language is applied sparsely – only single phrases or words (mostly in English) are used by the performers to inspire the audience's imagination.

The ensemble's work is based on an acute criticism of society, raising social issues, such as racism, gender prejudices, sexual hypocrisy and political pretension. By questioning the status quo and giving full credit to the imagined – trusting it as much as the experienced – the ensemble produces the energy that characterizes its work. It can be the energy of a burning fuse or that of a persistent, far-away flame.

劇団解体社
プロフィール

「身体の演劇」にこだわり、独特の演劇スタイル
を確立している劇団。寡黙にそしてラディカルな
肉体表現で、研ぎ澄まされた緊張感ある舞台を誕
生させている。

1985年〈場の演劇〉を開始。駅や路上、河原、
公園などで数々の野外劇を展開する。さらに観客
席を固定せず、一つの公演で上演場所を次々に変
えていく〈移動演劇〉—「遊行の景色」を発表。
以後、各地を巡演する。

1991年より「THE DOG」と題した〈密室劇〉
を開始。集団創造による多彩な演技メソッドを開
拓し、1993年東京・本郷にフリースペース「本
郷DOK」を開設。アメリカ公演を経て翌年
「THE DOG 三部作」を発表。

1995年より「TOKYO GHETTO」シリーズを
開始。東京を収容所都市と見立て、そこに住む
人々＝〈東京難民〉の営みをラディカルに綴るこ
のシリーズは、上演空間を様々に変えて展開し、
そのテーマや身体論は世界的視野に立つ演劇とし
て高い評価を得る。

1997年、「次世代のためのパフォーミングアーツ」
をコンセプトに、東京・湯島に「Free Space カ
ンバス」を開設。未来イメージと社会性を併せ持
つ新たな舞台ジャンルの創造に挑んでいる。また
メルボルンのカンパニー "NYID" とのコラボレー
ション・プロジェクト「Journey to Con-
Fusion」を1999年より始動。国際異文化交流
にも積極的に取り組んでいる。

2001年、これまでの活動の集大成となる新作
「バイバイ／未開へ」を携え、ハンブルグで行わ
れる LAOKOON Festival 2001 を皮切りに、
ワールドツアーを敢行。解体社が標榜する「身体
の演劇」が世界で今後どのように受け止められる
かが注目されている。

Gekidan KAITAISHA
SUMMARIZED BIOGRAPHY

Gekidan KAITAISHA (literally "Theatre of Deconstruction") was founded in 1985 by Artistic Director Shimizu Shinjin. In 1986, the Tokyo-based ensemble started to experiment with incorporating mise-en-scene into other genres: electronic music, film, visual arts, and object installations.

KAITAISHA developed and began presenting their theory of "Theatre of Place", utilizing different outdoor locations as performance spaces, such as city ruins, streets, river banks and parks. A "mobile theatre" performance called The Drifting View was staged. During the course of the performance the actors moved from one location to another. The play was invited to many cities as part of a series about transformation and breathing life into landscapes.

In 1991, KAITAISHA created the indoor performance series THE DOG.

As a result of their former outdoor performances, the group's theory of "Theatre of Place" had evolved to incorporate multifaceted dimensions.

The actors' power increased through new achievements, and the group attempted to shape their strength into a new crystallized style.

In 1995, TOKYO GHETTO, another indoor performance series, was initiated. The purpose of this production was to search for the remains of "bodies" of the theatre in the 1990s. The play's themes – non-fictionalism, political bodies and gender – received high international acclaim as theatre with a global perspective. In 1996, KAITAISHA was invited to the Eurokaz Festival in Croatia where the group caused a sensation and received rave reviews. TOKYO GHETTO was also performed in the UK, Germany and Korea in 1997.

The following year, Gekidan

KAITAISHA produced ZERO-CATEGORY and DE-CONTROL. Inspired by the motto "The performing arts for the next generation", they began creating a new genre incorporating images of the future to connect with society.

In 1999, KAITAISHA cooperated for the first time with another ensemble to create Journey to Con-Fusion. Their partner was Australian multi-media group NYID (Not Yet It's Difficult), known for performances in public spaces.

In Tokyo in 2001, the group created and premiered Bye-Bye: The New Primitive – a showcase of the company's artistic progress up to the present.
Initiated by an invitation of Kampnagel in Hamburg to participate in the opening of the LAOKOON festival 2001, KAITAISHA will be touring New York and Europe in autumn of 2001.

Photography 1991-2001

Photographs — Miyauchi Katsu

舞台写真 1991-2001
写真－宮内勝

THE DOG I - People in a foreign land
THE DOG I －異郷の子らー （1993）

◄ The Drifting View VI - Shining Heights
遊行の景色 VI －Shining Heights－ （1991）

THE DOG I - People in a foreign land
THE DOG I 一異郷の子らー（1993）

THE DOG I - People in a foreign land @Charlotte, U.S.A.
THE DOG I 一異郷の子らー（1993）

THE DOG I - People in a foreign land
THE DOG I 一異郷の子らー (1993)

The Drifting View VII - The Last Walk @Atlanta, U.S.A.
遊行の景色 VII －The Last Walk － (1993)

The Drifting View VII - The Last Walk　@Atlanta, U.S.A.
遊行の景色 VII －The Last Walk －（1993）

THE DOG I - People in a foreign land
THE DOG I ─異郷の子ら─（1994）

THE DOG II - A Little Story （1994）

THE DOG II - A Little Story （1994）

THE DOG III - Saint Orgie
THE DOG III ―聖オルギアー―（1994）

THE DOG III - Saint Orgie
THE DOG III ―聖オルギア―（1994）

TOKYO GHETTO - Voidness has gone, and the era of absurdity is coming.
TOKYO GHETTO －空虚は去り、愚劣の時代がやってくる－ （1995）

The Drifting View VIII - They have no name
遊行の景色 VIII ―彼女らに名前はない― (1995)

The Drifting View VIII - They have no name
遊行の景色 VIII ―彼女らに名前はない― （1995）

The Proscenium - TOKYO GHETTO（1995）

The Proscenium - TOKYO GHETTO（1995）

◀TOKYO GHETTO - Orgie
 TOKYO GHETTO －オルギアー （1995）

TOKYO GHETTO III - Dying Anarchy
TOKYO GHETTO III －瀕死のアナーキーー （1996）

TOKYO GHETTO - Lullaby @Zlatar Bistrica, Croatia
TOKYO GHETTO －ララバイー （1996）

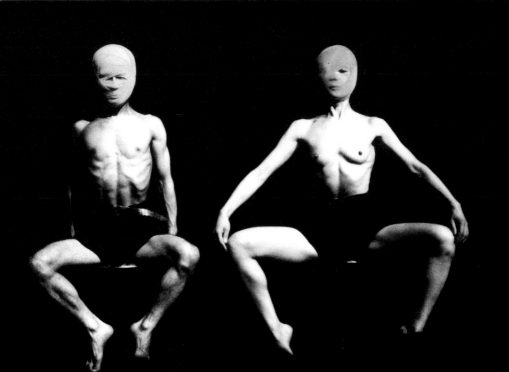

TOKYO GHETTO - Orgie @Zagreb, Croatia（1996）

TOKYO GHETTO - Orgie ＠Zagreb, Croatia（1996）

TOKYO GHETTO - L'é puisé　＠Pula, Croatia
TOKYO GHETTO －消尽－（1996）

TOKYO GHETTO - HARD CORE ▶
TOKYO GHETTO －ハード・コアー（1996）

TOKYO GHETTO - Class in Twilight @Cardiff, Wales, UK
TOKYO GHETTO －薄明の階級－ （1997）

TOKYO GHETTO - Orgie#2 @Bristol, England, UK（1997）

The Proscenium - TOKYO GHETTO @Seoul, Korea (1997)

ZERO CATEGORY
零カテゴリー（1997）

ZERO CATEGORY
零カテゴリー（1997）

ZERO CATEGORY II - The Season of New Abjection
零カテゴリーII ― The Season of New Abjection ―（1998）

DE-CONTROL I - Cluster/Act in the Cell
DE-CONTROL I 一群れ／独房アクト— (1999)

◀ DE-CONTROL @Melbourne, Australia (1999)

DE-CONTROL IV - Iconoclastic Arena
DE-CONTROL IV 一イコノクラスティック・アリーナー（1999）

Bye-Bye : Into the Century of Degeneration
バイバイ 一退化の世紀へー （1999）

◀ DE-CONTROL II - Neuro System
DE-CONTROL II 一 Neuro 系一 （1999）

Bye-Bye : Into the Century of Degeneration
バイバイ ー退化の世紀へー (1999)

Bye-Bye : Into the Century of Degeneration
バイバイ －退化の世紀へ－ （1999）

Journey to Con-Fusion 2
混成への旅 2 （2000）

◄ DE-CONTROL V - many many （2000）

Bye-Bye: The New Primitive
バイバイ／未開へ（2001）

Bye-Bye: The New Primitive
バイバイ／未開へ（2001）

Bye-Bye: The New Primitive
バイバイ／未開へ（2001）

Bye-Bye: The New Primitive
バイバイ／未開へ（2001）

The Birth of a Theatre and the Besieged Body:
A Strategy for Globalization

A Dialogue between Otori Hidenaga and Shimizu Shinjin

Photographs — Miyauchi Katsu

Part I

Shimizu Shinjin   Otori Hidenaga

O : Today I would like to talk about what is being considered when we think of theatre as a form of representation, within a fundamental discussion about issues in theatre. What if we look at matters like what form can be established when theatre is questioned as a concrete representation? In order to do so, first we have to talk about what has been emerging and subsiding over the past decade. I'm thinking that theatre artists and critics in the 1990s have been discovering much the same thing. For instance, in 1988, the Polish director Tadeusz Kantor (1915-1990) observed, "There is Something that is manifested only when one is faced with the END." (in the essay "To Save from Oblivion") Only towards the end of the 1980s did Kantor himself come to realize the significance of the mark he had left in the world. Only then did he become aware of the fact that his Theatre of Death was intimately related to the wars of the twentieth century. He grasped this more clearly and sharply than when he was writing his Manifesto of Theatre of Death. His theatre was a response to Theodor Adorno's comment that "to write lyric poetry after Auschwitz is barbarous." (in "Prismen-Kulturkritik und Gesellshaft" 1955) Around the end of the 1980s, various writers had started to experience such a realization. Incidentally, it was in 1984 or '85 that you began searching for a new direction in theatre practice wasn't it?

S : Yes. I began with Mobile Outdoor Theatre in the Hinoemata Performance Festival. This performance series was called "The Drifting View."

O : So you began with outdoor work at Hinoemata in 1985. Previously, you had been doing shows in closed rooms. It was around 1985 when you started exploring

The Drifting View @ Hinoemata Performance Festival (1985)

Outdoor Theatre in locations like fields and river-beds. Of course, to some degree you were working without really grasping its significance. But, as you gained experience, you began to reconsider the significance of this transformation in your theatre. And I believe it was then that you first came to realize a kind of historical awareness in connection with this movement.

In the 1990s, KAITAISHA was offered more opportunities to perform abroad. On a practical level, you've been experiencing the transformation of theatre by performing in different spaces for differing audiences. Amidst this sequence of activities, what have you been thinking as a director? Have you had any key experiences? What's the significance of the 1990s in your history of directing? How do you reflect on it from the present of 2001? I believe these matters are important for theatre. So, first of all, can you tell me how you as an artist have observed this transformation in theatre over the past 15 to 20 years? Also, please say something about what you have been trying to do. You could respond to these questions directly if you like, although it's not necessary.

Theatre of Images and the Body as a Medium:

S : Well -- the 1980s, right? I might jump from one point to another, since I have various memories entangled in each other. The reason why I started doing Outdoor Theatre was because as a starting point I wanted to literally go out of the theatre. At that time, it was very hard for me to sit in the audience and watch what we call the Little Theater. I would get rather overwhelmed by the waves of remorseful recollections and sentiments. I realized then, that it would be impossible for us to advance if we were to remain in the same arena with these people. Our theatre was too similar to these small theatres, especially in the area of acting. Well, I thought, if that's the case, we have no recourse but to change the various conditions our theatre depends upon along with the performance style which holds these conditions intact. In short, we decided to make "acting" impossible. Ordinarily, if you hear about an outdoor play, you might think it's a performance on an outdoor stage. However in such cases, the only difference is whether the theatre is indoors or outdoors. Outdoor Theatre, as I conceived and formulated it, was something entirely different from that. First of all, there were no audience seats, nor any stage. It could happen in daytime or at night. Both the audience and the actors would move along with the performance, which meant there was no fixed performance space. It might be in a park, in a river-bed, on the street, at a train station, or beside an abandoned ruin. It was an effort in which actors and audience attempted to manifest theatrical events. And it was during this very period of time that we encountered the problem of "the body." In the midst of these vast, freewheeling, chaotic circumstances, we discovered we could neither dance nor act! We could not possibly draw on pre-existing acting techniques that involve gushing emotions and large-as-life naturalism. What was invoked instead, was "Theatre of Images" supported theoretically by notions of "the body as object" or "the body as a medium".

The Gulf War and The Death of Aesthetics:

For instance, if one places a body (the per-former) as an infinitely foreign substance in the midst of a familiar landscape (the space), and then there's some collective body such as a train arriving at a station, people walking on the pedestrian bridge and cars pulling away, then we see all of them differently through that one body (placed in their midst). The audience expe-riences a transformation of perception of a landscape it ought to be familiar with, to a perception renewed and reborn as the per-formance progresses. At that time, I was really drawn to methods that used the body as an opportunity for perceptual transfor-mation. I was planning to expand this type of performance by shaping it as we trav-eled, doing it outdoors, moving the audi-ence physically or by using technological art. These ideas were bankrupted when the Gulf War broke out in 1991. All my moti-vations disappeared instantly. I guess that was real bankruptcy. So I shut myself in to wrestle with issues surrounding the body and the power that besieges it. Practically this meant continuous practice in "walking" with the actors in our warehouse rehearsal space in Kawasaki with no performing for two years! (laughs)

O : In a sense, this method of Theater of Images of the 1980s - replacing the body as a theatrical image to transform the space - is aesthetic isn't it? And for you, it was the Gulf War that made you realize this point at issue.

S : The political element was minimal. Or rather, there were certain circumstances or language constraints that prevented the political element from surfacing, as in "the Global Village" and (Marshall) McLuhan. Media technology gradually differentiates people's desires in a homogenized world. This is nothing but Theatre of Images, right? It encompasses the varieties of body, music, art, and ethnicity within an overall concept of "total theatre," that con-tinuously strives for new aesthetic compo-sitions to accelerate the consumption of images.

What the Gulf War clarified was that such differentiated desires can be unified. Diversity is affirmed as long as power does not come to the surface. But when power is invoked and exercised, it easily unifies the world at once, by information control and crisis management. For precisely this reason it is possible to say that Theatre of Images can be politicized. For instance, the body used in Theatre of Images essen-tially has no aim or objective. It doesn't involve the perspective of a subject work-ing toward self-realization. The body is simply a part of the whole and a medium for establishing a relationship. It is physi-cality that gets foregrounded by the rela-tionship between the body and space, objects, or whatever else is there. I present "the body as a battlefield" through a process of reinterpreting this relationship in a political context and rearranging it in terms of power structures. These were the thoughts in my head that led to a series of performances at "Hongo DOK".

O : I'm wondering why it was the Gulf War that was the trigger for these thoughts? I mean, around that period of time, I think there were several major events besides the Gulf War, like Sarajevo in 1993 and the Fall of the Berlin Wall in 1989, which could have equally made you to expose the body as a battlefield. It's natural that such a moment of realization is different for each person but why was it the Gulf War for you? You mentioned McLuhan, maybe it's related to that. Could you elaborate on this point?

Theatre is a Battlefield:

S : Basically, I regard theatre as "war". It's truly war, in the sense that a human body is indiscriminately consumed (in war). However, there was no body in the Gulf War. It was such a shock for theatre, that a war without bodies had raised the curtain of the 1990s. That is one reason.
The other is related to globalization by the media. I'm talking about television here. Massive amounts of information were being broadcast. Anyone and everyone was inundated with media images from television. I also realized that what I called "my own intuition" had vanished as well.

O : Naturally. As you were saying, war is related to theatre through the connective phrase "the body as a battlefield." If I may digress a little, the Gulf War gave the impression that it was manipulated by media technology. Among several literary works being discussed at that time was (Jean) Baudrillard's "The Gulf War Did Not Take Place" (La Guerre du Golfe n'a pas eu lieu, 1991). To sum it up, he proposes that the perception of the Gulf War as a form of battle occurring in a hyper-real space dominated the media, hence the loss and concealment of the body. Such a formulation was implicit in the Gulf War victory. However, bombs were actually being dropped and oil fields were being destroyed by the multi-national forces. At that time, the press was thoroughly controlled. For instance, on TV we incessantly saw two water birds smeared black with oil which was pouring out of the oil field destroyed by the Iraqi army. People throughout the world saw only these two birds, but we were made to believe that all water-birds were black with oil. In this kind of manipulation, you recognize what was suppressed and hidden from us, so to speak. I think it's important to consider what significance this phenomenon held in your activities as a director in the 1990s. Furthermore, in connecting this phenomenon to representation, what does it mean when it is represented by a theatre artist, as opposed to a visual artist, a writer, or film maker? For instance, in what way do you see the Gulf War being related to your approach of 'the body as a battlefield'? Can you talk about that?

S : It is, after all, imagination. This might sound a bit unrefined, but we must re-train our imagination. The corpses of Iraqi soldiers were definitely buried alive in that desert that we saw on our TV screens. I can't imagine what kind of body it was and what kind of meaning was attached to it. But I can't help being drawn to such a body, I mean a human body. In relation to theatre history, ever since Modernism, the body has ceased to be a vessel to express someone's character. It has been reduced to physical elements such as velocity or body temperature or weight. It has become the locus of data. As a result, we can only see a human body as a number and a quantity. If we look back, this was first seen in World War I. War in the twentieth century discovered conversion techniques which turned bodies into materials, quantities, data. The consequence of which is the corpses of Iraqi soldiers buried in the desert, which we now are unable to count. They're lying there, it seems to me, like "vanished shells".

O : Well it's not that you have actually seen them, so there are still just an infinite number of corpses in your imagination right? The situation of the collection of corpses in such a place, I think it would be possible to call a human condition, which you then make a reality.

S : Yes, I stage it.

O : You stage it. When you stage it, you have real actors. That means that their bodies will appear on stage. How do you realize your imagination in them? Do the actors appear on the stage representing corpses of Iraqi soldiers?

S : No, that's impossible. It is impossible to represent. That is why I had to consider representation as a fundamental problem. It is not like explaining some specific incident, or replacing it with something else that demonstrates the act. This won't unveil the concealed body. No, what I was wondering was whether an original event gets repeated during a specific action, in the midst of exe-

cuting that action?

O : You mean a repetition of form?

S : Or rather, a form exists first, although it is perhaps somewhat chaotic. For example, say I'm talking about a particular picture, a movie, a painting, or a text with the actors. I start creating a form from there. However, this is still no more than mere gesture amidst daily life as it is. No word helps. There has to be some definite event, in order to make it representative.

O : You mean what happened in Iraq?

S : No, that's not it.

O : What, then?

S : As a simple example, there is an exercise called "Restriction" in our movement training. An actor literally presses down the upper body of another actor: it is bound. It is bound and released again and again. When we repeated this exercise, one actress started escaping from the restriction in a very strange manner. It always happened in one particular scene, and it always happened to this particular actress in the particular restriction exercise. After rehearsal I asked her the reason. She said, "My first memory was that I learned how to write from my mother. She guided my right hand with her right hand. But I couldn't write the word 'Ma'. Then my mother got upset and said, "Ma' is the word for mama, so you have to learn it no matter what! I won't forgive you.' Then she pressed down on my body." Such a memory, presumably which she had suppressed thirty years ago, was evoked and repeated in this movement. I'm wondering if I can actualize a representation as such an event, such a situation. Given that I cannot represent the corpse of an Iraqi soldier, can I compete with that by utilizing the actor's inability to achieve representation?

O : So you are not representing what happened in Iraq are you?

S : No. It's impossible.

O : But you are thinking about it.

S : Such an idea cannot come to my mind unless I'm thinking about it.

O : In other words, even if you are thinking about it, you're not reproducing it, because it's impossible to reproduce via representation. The issue here is the form of representation, which confronts it -- and which, I suppose, cannot really be called "its representation." When you attempt to accomplish an action in the face of the untenability of representation, the problem of representation comes to light.

S : Such representation has to resonate with what's happening in the world at this very moment.

O : In short, you engage in the representation of the situation in Iraq by being involved in the impossibility of representation?

S : Yes.

Representing the Impossibility of Representation:

S : I'm repeating myself here, but it's an issue of imagination. We have to activate our political imagination in regard to what's happening in the world, what's being concealed, and what kind of body is being imprisoned. In terms of the necessary attitude for that, now is not the time to maintain the same theory and method constructed from a transcendent vantage-point. Especially when you tour abroad, you have to keep close contact with contingencies and rearrange the structure of your work all the time, on the spot. The significance of the specifics of a particular work is no longer important. The universality of the work no longer exists. This was our experience, for example, in Croatia a couple of years ago. It's a place where a machine-gun jumps out at you from the boot of a normal car. How do you deal with the impossibility of representation in such a place? You cannot fall back onto stereotypes and conventions. In a place where refugees are right there in the suburban hills, how can you relate to that situation, unless you can break through the perceptual boundaries of the situation?

What Globalization Exposes:

O : If that's the case, and you try to do it in Japan, we have the problem of subject matter, since we don't have refugees like Zagreb does. You made mention of what might be concealed by the word "globalization", but conversely, some things may be exposed by it. Many different problems are exposed and concealed in various forms. It's often the case when we talk about globalization that homogenization is raised as an issue. On the other hand, it sometimes exposes the existence of differences. Artists have to respond to that. For instance, Professor Arjun Appadurai from the University of Chicago raises the relationship between globalization and urban culture as an issue; from this he draws out an argument regarding the dilemma of the restroom in Bombay. In short, what globalization brought into question in the city of Bombay, was the system of hygiene and the dilemma of the public amenity. The dilemma of the public toilet must have existed in the slums of Bombay for a long time, but it surfaced as an urgent issue in light of globalization. This is a problem almost impossible to solve. Still, a project to build restrooms one by one was conceived. While it may be solved in the distant future, it presents a difficult dilemma. What one notes here is that homeless people in Japan don't confront the same issue of public toilets. They live in parks where they can use public toilets. Furthermore, while homelessness is a problem, whether it's a major dilemma or not is uncertain. There must be much more formidable problems in Japan, only it's not clear as to what they are. For instance, the problem of the refugees in suburban Zagreb is a kind of exposed problem, I think. When you perform in Zagreb, you respond to that. I'm not saying that it's easy, but what do you try to respond to when you perform in Japan? What exists as a problem? What do you try to plug in, in terms of the problematic in Japanese culture which might

exist as the impossibility of representation? The question is what the 'body as a battle-field' should be connected with, isn't it?

S : To put it simply, it is violence imposed on the body. Regarding my method of structuring performances, initially I expose the violent gaze which besieges the body. Exposed to direct examination, the power structure becomes rough. As soon as this occurs, media images strip away and reconstruct the structure. The body is concealed and the structure prevails suspended in mid-air - reactionary restrictions, brainwashing, disciplinary training...

O : Could you be more specific?

Origins of Domestic Violence:

S : For example, in my directing there is a signature scene of violence which these days most audiences equate with domestic violence and maltreatment. I would like to see this change in audience reaction as progress. It was not regarded that way a couple of years ago. When they saw the actress being pummelled and her back becoming blood-red, they would say things like "the marks look like angel's wings," or they felt the pulse of life in the rhythm of the beatings. (laughs) However, on the other hand, there's an impulsive reaction to fervently attribute this violence to individual human nature. They consider the cause of this violence a "darkness of the mind." This darkness of the mind is so elusive! How is it possible to comprehend the mental condition which is quite literally "darkness"?! (laughs) Why is critical domestic violence more prevalent than the violence we knew of in the past, such as husband and wife quarrels, or the strict disciplining (of a child)? The structure that produces domestic violence must be questioned and criticized in performance. That is what theatre should do.

O : To put it plainly, can we say it's a product of globalization?

S : Yes. And its' breeding ground is capitalism and the nation. On one hand, it encourages dismembering families. On the other hand, it parasitizes them. We are all aware of such hollow mechanisms. It isn't something which lies in (individual) "darkness."

O : If that's the case, it's extremely important how one responds to the condition of globalization or how one opposes it. In a sense, globalization is currently popular, while contemporary artists are looking for ways to deal with it. For instance, in the case of Japan, in the midst of globalization there is rising nationalism, which means excluding the outside, or the others.

S : Yes, racism is hidden in the shadows.

O : Globalization may have been conceived to allow for the possibility of differentiation, disruption, and individualism. But the reality under capitalism is the development of racialism by restricting select individual areas of movement by access-deprivation, thereby forcing a homogeneous norm. Thus, in the end it becomes apparent that power has come to control the body even more tightly.

S : It is like those campaign slogans which incite fear and hatred. They are encouraging us to supervise and rule more, as if they were Volunteer Self-Defense Forces.

O : It is for this reason that Japanese theatre is becoming more conservative.

S : As is often said, imminent opposition to globalization is hyper-nationalism. Hyper-nationalism sounds new, but actually it was known as imperialism in the past. The other thing is fundamentalism. Neither of these are an option for Japan, so nationalism begins to emerge. The reality is that, the "Japanese art revival" consists of a return to recent mysticism. Apart from works in other genres which have received attention, as far as theatre is concerned, it can never achieve success going in that direction. To be honest, it makes me squirm to think about a reactionary so-called National Theatre being critically regarded in the international theatre market, which under globalisation is thriving as art tourism.

Takuhon Cultural Entertainment and Japan:

O : You are an isolated figure within the overall current of Japanese theatre. In Japan a huge project has been developed to create the theatre for the nation. The 1997 opening of the New National Theatre (Hatsudai, Tokyo) devoted to modern theatre was not simply a celebratory event. There had been a strong movement in the 1990s in support of this opening. With this theatre as the leader, Japanese contemporary theatre began developing based on exceedingly nationalistic and parochial values. The fact that it was realized in 1997 epitomizes the developments in theatre in the 1990s. The theatre has hardly any links with the outside world. Even in dramas which use war as a motif, the problem of war is staged completely from a domestic view, in the same way Kato Norihiro addresses the problem of war-responsibility and ethics as a domestic problem in his "Post-Defeat Theory." For instance, Kaneshita Tatsuo wrote a play set in a concentration camp in the Philippines. But only Japanese people appear in the story in this Philippine concentration camp. This phenomenon is also found in "The Burmese Harp". This kind of insular sensibility has become a reality. The inter-communication with the world made possible by globalization, has come to naught. Most plays employ this approach. In its' endeavours to represent the reality of Japan, theatre is making a commitment to pop-phenomena, if anything. People call this Takuhon culture.

S : What does that mean?

O : Takuhon is a paper print on stone. If you place a piece of paper on the surface of a tombstone and tap it a couple of times, the letters are transposed to the surface of the paper. This kind of theatre doesn't deeply analyze and commit itself to the reality, it copies it like a Takuhon. You can tell whenever you see it. For instance, the theatre of Kerarino Sandrovich's Nylon 100 ℃ company is Takuhon cultural entertainment. Here, you'll encounter a girl who you think you would actually meet if you were to go to a place like the reality in which she exists. Or a modern family is depicted, which you imagine might really exist somewhere in reality. However, it is, so to speak, a duplicated reality, like Takuhon, made into a sequence of scenic entertainments. I cannot possibly imagine that it produces anything that activates theatre or stimulates one's mind.

The Paradox of Tragedy and Dignity:

Theatre is a response to reality. For instance, Greek theatre was a response to reality. It portrays Oedipus' destruction, as the Gods' oracles foretold. Oedipus' tragedy lies in that he lives as the Gods predicted. However, according to Walter Benjamin's "The Origin of German Tragic Drama", it is wrong to only see this as human defeat. He argues that Oedipus defeats the Gods. Strangely, when watching Oedipus, the Greek audience disapproved of and rejected the schemes of the Gods. This decision is what's crucial. In short, Greek tragedy exists as the place to reject the Gods whose orders controlled Greek civilisation. In depicting a human figure being destroyed by those orders they are rejecting the Gods. The nobility of Greek tragedy lies in the paradoxical appearance of the human figure. And it is when such a powerless human being rejects the Gods, despite their overwhelming advantage, that the Gods' fall begins. I see the possibility for theatre in the structure underlying this apparent tragedy. The 'impossibility of representation' problem is related to this. In short, in the reality of Japan, one's awareness of the impossibility of representation when representing is the issue. Recently, in the Festival de Théâtre des Amériques in Montreal, I saw a play with which I was fairly impressed. It kept me surprised for seven hours while watching it. It was a play about massacre called "Rwanda '94," which a collective called Groupov in Belgium created with a community in Rwanda. It was a work which raised the 'impossibility of representation' and the matter of decision for deliberation.

Limitations of Representation and the Theatre of Testimony:

Belgium is the nation which had ruled in Rwanda. After it returned Rwanda to independence, racial conflict re-ignited. This was one of the precipitating causes of the massacre. Some survived it. At the beginning of this play, one of these survivors testifies as to what she witnessed. She does not tell us how to solve this problem, she only tells us what she has seen. The group went to Rwanda to collect various testimonies and to investigate the facts of the situation. They acquired various resources, materials, and documents and in the actual performance showed us footage of the massacre recorded secretly. Several texts, like the testimonies of the dead were also presented, to which people respond by saying it was not a good idea to expose such materials in public. Then a newscaster called BBB says, "No, we must see them," and systematically pursues an illumination of the facts. We watch and hear the progress

as the play develops. We come to learn the facts of a massacre that couldn't be prevented, in great detail. No solutions for the prevention of the massacre are suggested. But what's important here is what we think. That is to say, in our overwhelming powerlessness we make a collective decision to renounce massacres. Theatre exists as the place for this decision. But it is done in tandem with someone's testimony. Survivors convey the voices of the dead in their stead. This is nothing other than the construction of history. It is the Greeks who discovered that testimony, as the construction of history and fundamental disapproval, are the very things achieved in theatrical space. This is the power of theatre that the significant theatre artists of the twentieth century have conveyed to us. People like Tadeusz Kantor definitely created such theatre.

This form of theatre approaches the impossibility of representation in its connection with 'Testimony'. Significant theatre in the twentieth century was established with the trigger of testimony. Kantor himself often said, "The dead testify." As one possibility for contemporary theatre, I'm thinking of the theatre as a place for testimonies which turn the past into history. As I listen to you, it seems that you also are involved in theatre which aims to do so.

S : Yes, this is what I have to do.

O : I've been engaged with plans for the LAOKOON Festival 2002, happening in Hamburg next year. I'm wondering about "History and Memory" as a unified theme. (Walter) Benjamin's "Awakening" will be the pivotal idea which Kantor said, "Something that is manifested only when one is faced with the END." However, we already passed the year 2000 and are now in 2001. We are standing at the beginning. Therefore, I think we need to shift our awareness a little. We're about to wake to 2001. If that's the case, what will we recall from the first moment of awakening? In the moment of awakening, the dreams we remember will be quickly forgotten. How can we analyze them and fix them before we do so? Is this itself not the work of history? I think it may well become a key motif for thought in contemporary theatre. That's because the performance of theatre in the "contemporaneous present" also means placing the past into the present and critically rearranging it. I'm thinking about the body you were talking about a little while ago, and the story of an actress who couldn't write the character for "Ma." I wonder if the situation which came from work like this can be connected with the testimonies of survivors.

The Trap of Confession:

S : Yes, it can. However, you would need a new approach to connect them. Otherwise, even if it's expressed on stage it

ZERO CATEGORY @Tokyo Metropolitan Art Space (1997)

ends up becoming a confession. How can we connect this confession with testimony? This very "how" is in question. We will probably talk about this in a more concrete fashion in the later section of work analysis... but now I can tell you that the reason why the circuit of confession to testimony appears to be broken is because the body is deprived. "The body" is deprived of its owner - the only one who is supposed to be to be able to tell the truth. It is of course achieved by media images. For instance, you mentioned Rwanda a little while ago, which I saw via satellite broadcast.

O : You mean the incident in Rwanda itself?

S : It was about the investigation of reasons why the massacre occurred, through testimonies of people involved. I think it was in 1997. I remember it well, partly because I used some of the voices in the performance of "Zero Category."

O : It wasn't a play?

S : No, it wasn't. It was a documentary film called "The Tragedy of Rwanda," produced by a Canadian television station. What shocked me most was the sight of a prison. A massive number of people had been captured. Their cells were so small they couldn't lie down. They had to urinate at their feet while standing. The scars in their feet would rot and turn necrotic. Many people had to have their rotten feet amputated, and collapsed on the spot. Television cameras shot the spectacle. Of course no one uttered a word although one man tore off his rotting big toe and threw it at the camera. The television programme showed this sight to us. Recently also, a documentary film about the massacre in Bosnia was aired. It included detailed materials such as testimonies from the Dutch army officers on the front, who had been the core of the United Nations Forces. These officers withdrew and returned to their own country, even though they knew that it surely meant the massacre of these refugees. One testimony of such an officer was filled with bitterness. He started out saying something like, "At that time . . ." just like an actor says his lines. I see this is as confession. Not a single word from the voices of the people concerned, the victims, nor the survivors, who really should testify. These people are always seen just standing in utter amazement. There were voices here and there in the Bosnia one, but the Rwanda film had only pictures, not a single word...anyway. I'm often driven to screaming, "Please say something!", but it's always the same picture of them just standing there. If you depicted this situation as "Cattle before the slaughter", it would be understood but it will never reach the level of representation. These bodies are not "poetry". They are not literary phenomenon. If I may borrow your phrase Mr Otori, I think the bodies just as they are, standing in overwhelming powerlessness are the testimonies themselves. Testimony cannot be explained in speech or words. However, we can salvage testimony by directing our gaze to the body, or by sifting the imagination in situations of repetition. I earnestly hope to continue developing these methods more and more.

Part II

O : So far we've talked about principles: how artists regard this world and when they make their works how they bridge their techniques of recognition and expression. So, let's change our focus to Kaitaisha's works performed during the nineties. You have said that since the Gulf War you have come to think "Theatre of Images" means an imperialist or capitalist way of suppressing human beings. That's one very important concern, and secondly, your works are actually changing aren't they? In your own analysis, what do you think such changes are about?

S : Ok. I'll reply in the context of our productions "THE DOG" and "TOKYO GHETTO".
As I said earlier, "THE DOG" was the first performance after a two year silence in which we gained new members and made a new studio at Hongo (Tokyo). I think you can say we came from the outdoors to a closed room. That was 1993, the year we went to the States. At that time, I used to think only two things; how do I amputate "Theatre of Images"(from our work), and the political nature of the body. "TOKYO GHETTO" was first performed in 1995 and toured to Europe and Korea. Its theme was how to represent human bodies exposed to violence. In method I'd become more aware of "deconstruction" or "inner-breaking" as a way of performing. Why was this work so provocative to European spectators at that time? I would like to summarise this now.

Performance, Violence, Provocation:

O : What was so provocative?

S : It was the direct use of human bodies for violence. A man actually beat the back of a woman for as long as he could physically endure. He continued to beat her for 20 minutes.

O : Violence used as the beating of another's body?

S : This is a prohibited thing. Within European stage expression, violence is only suggested, is just represented.

O : They don't actually hit on stage.

S : On the stage, usually violence is only suggested/represented. I've seen the action of sex on stage and people cutting their own bodies. But presenting this kind of violence on stage, of one body to another in a way so as to incur suitable damage, is taboo.

O : To speak conventionally, in hitting scenes you hit your own hand right? This is the way used in most movie or dramas, but you actually hit.

S : Yes, I tried to show through the scene I spoke of, the possibility of non-fictionalism. The fact of beating and the action of continuous beating until its limit; meaning the very fact and its continuous action, and that's all. I made a stage consisting of only these two things: facts and actions. One of

the most important things as a director was not to give the spectators any explanations about these actions. I didn't show any reasons, motives or factors which would account for why he beat her. I made it impossible to judge cause-effect and good-bad until the theatre was full of living anxiety.

When I think about it now, this approach may have been the reason why this work was so provocative. At any rate, violence and anxiety, as I was told on tour, has a positive function and can communicate in relation to the global representation of theatre. And another thing was Orientalism.

O : Asia!?

S : No, Orient. I thought the boundary between East and West no longer existed.

O : You mean, they have it but you don't?

From East-West to South-North:

S : Yes, I presented the boundary between South and North.

O : Its a little hard to understand what you are saying, so I will ask a little more precisely. You mean to say the notion of human bodies as it were, exists as part of a system, and more importantly, you are trying to figure out how to manipulate that. Perhaps if you share your thoughts about the meaning behind the various techniques you have employed in this context...

S : Movement.

O : If you think in terms of movement, whether it be the bodies of Noh or Kabuki, or the Butoh body, I would guess that they are all different. But those stages have come about over a long period by thinking about the body of the actor.

S : No, they're the same. Everyone is saying the same thing.

O : So, it isn't different to what I was saying right, is that what you mean?

S : For example, Zeami's "Hana"(flower), Artaud's "Double", "Hakusei"(Taxidermy) of Hijikata Tatsumi, Kecak, Kathakali, "Contraction" of Martha Graham, Contact Improvisation, Classical Ballet, Forsythe's "Neglected bodies", all of them have grown from one shared root. They are all related to incest. In other words, they are fundamentally based on whether it is possible to move without prohibition.
Yes, Artaud said "Human beings aren't created well, there is no order, harmony, nor anything." Hijikata communicated "Being born is an improvisation". Basically I interpret what he means, for humans being born is a system. That's what I hear. As Adorno says, "I am without doubt living the age of Enlightenment". However, my body, the contemporary body, whichever way you see it, is only being lived as a result of (the) Enlightenment. Therefore, the aim of freeing the human body means transforming oneself into a living thing other than 'human' and unpacking formalised movement processes. Obviously others have also done this work.

O : So you're saying there's nothing unique to Noh or Kabuki. And even aside from Noh and Kabuki, that Martha Graham and classical Ballet are doing the same thing. In fact you're saying all have body representation in common. In this sense, East-West thinking is problematic isn't it.

S : Geo-politically speaking, this boundary has already been discarded. Since the Cold War era there has been a USA-Russian space strategy. Currently the body is the point of contact in the theatre-site of cultural practice. Cultural boundaries are being strongly recognised in order to protect cultural identity.
I am speaking not only of Europe but it was something I felt last year in Hong-Kong as well. Anyway, this desire for restoring "stability" must be rejected.

O : I see. So is the idea that "East and West" becomes insignificant as the problem of South-North emerges?

S : Its class-division, the separation of classes.

O : Can you speak a little more about the relationships between the South-North problem and the body?

The Asian Body Myth:

S : Its a problem of how to connect the theatrical act of repetition with the impossibility of expressing the Rwandan refugee problem, which is related politically and historically to confession and testimony.
Let me recall an event, was it 1995, at the

opening performance of "TOKYO GHET-TO". I remember your impression when you saw the bodies of the actresses. You said," (they look like) the Joy Division for the Japanese military!" This made me a bit bolder, as they had done nothing but sit for some time on stools. And at that time, quite a few overseas producers had begun to visit our studio. Most of them didn't appear too pleased. Someone said, "What I want to see is Asian kindness!"

In Asia, there's been events like the Nanking Massacre and the Sahako (Pol Pot's concentration camps). Ignoring this is worrisome. These events must not be forgotten. It is an artist's responsibility not to allow a structure capable of producing such events to go unchallenged.

My stage becomes quieter, and more than before, the bodies are exposed. I am dealing with naked bodies. The materiality of bodies - sweat, weight, skin, blood, tears - which I thought I had discarded when I returned to the studio. How do I relate them to history?

And yet again, the other thing I become aware of is "Theatre of Images". I said earlier "trans-nationalism" was in opposition to globalization. In spite of this, at the risk of being contradictory, I have begun to think of Theatre of Images as a possibility.

O : Do you think it is advantageous?

S : Yes, because it's trans-nationalism, from the view of Theatre of Images.

O : So for you trans-nationalism is an image.

S : Everybody is in closed spaces dig-ging holes in various ways in the hope of self-realization. Actually, they are only appearing to dig. But these bodies are actually just parts of the overall structure. As I pointed out before, these bodies will always be mediums or objects.

Returning to our earlier discussion, power and force are the things that have been intentionally erased. Especially, in the prevailing structure of Theatre of Images, in most cases it happens with no compulsion from anyone. In this way, each body appears independent or free, presenting a world in which spectators imagine people moving by their own will.

This isn't easily criticised, as "Peace" is stated as the goal while politics and power relations are ignored.

No one can speak ill of autonomy or peace, and so, this system is world-wide. In answer to the Theatre of Images I say "Wars are the result of aiming for peace".

Collapsing Borders and Borderlessness:

O : In this regard, Theatre of Images is linked to the myth of the universality of theatrical representation. That is to say, theatre can be understood all over the world. So someone says, "this theatre is universal." That means, for example this superb theatre is not only understood by Japanese but also by Americans, and will even have value in Africa. This method of making immutable myths relevant to all is where Theatre of Images comes in.

So, unlike the written language of conventional theatre, Theatre of Images doesn't use much language. Although I'm sure there is a locality even in a language of images as well.

When people say dance is easier to understand than theatre when looking at it for the first time, or when they use the word "borderless" without much thought, the notion of Theatre of Images as global is being celebrated. But actually, people began to recognise in the 90s that this situation must be criticised.

S : Yes, in my way there is nothing but "kaitai" (deconstruction). In order to criticise I used to create functional disorder from within the structure - the way of inner collapse. But that is far from enough. Something must be "amputated".

I used to think the various elements such as light, object, voice, picture slicing through the space as "Amputation" but I misunderstood this as scenographic construction. But it's not, it's not that... it's "meaning" that is desired. It is "meaning" that amputates Theatre of Images, or it could be called language. At that time, "meaning" for me meant Article 9 of the Japanese Constitution and Gender.

I used them for duration, the duration of the standard image until its limit, at which the point to "amputate" would come.

Bodies with AIDS:

O : In relation to the States of 1980s, theatre was very politicised, in '88-'89 in particular. "Politics of representation" was often used in those days, so it became very important to practitioners to express and problematize how they made their works in the relation to reality and cultural issues.

For those on stage it was also an important issue.

For example, the problem of how directors and others deal with bodies which are actually collapsing inside. Numbers of these people were on the increase in cities everywhere, relatives, people close to you, performers on stage, or even you yourself, all of which changed how human bodies were seen. Reza Abdoh (1963-1995), who died in 1995, said that the first thing he did when he first recognised he had AIDS was to look at his excretions. He began to look at his excretions differently to the way he had seen them before.

Excretions come out from the inside and are, as it were, both inner and outer parts of the body. He scrutinised them closely, their texture, shape, colour, and their viscosity. It was a turning point. The change in the way of seeing his own excretions was a point of departure for a change in seeing his entire body and so too, other bodies. Since coming to exist in this state, when making his performances, physical states of the performers became very important. In his theatre the exposed body received special attention. His theatre in 1988 and 1989 and into the 1990s was closely related to the contemporary human state. So the physical state of people itself had become the site of theatre.

Therefore the collapse of Theatre of Images started from the inside, from its technique of expressivity. It was an important issue for artists whether they noticed the breakdown of the theatre of images, or if they subscribed to it. I don't think when you recognise this phenomenon is the issue. I think the recognition of the issue is the most important point. You said, "I amputate by meaning". So does Reza Abdoh, whose productions look like Theatre of Images. With his spectacular productions Abdoh is regarded as the Robert Wilson of his generation. He made formative works on a very large scale.

S : Was it in a proscenium?

O : He used factory-like locations. In seeing photos from those productions, I had the impression they also had been amputated by meaning from the Theatre of Images. I think this was seen and felt by many directors during the transition from 1980s to 1990s, when the world was progressing toward a critical state. This time, as you were saying in relation to the Gulf War, was your turning point. Although Abdoh died in 1995, I think things had already begun to change. Including the things you have mentioned, how have you come to appreciate those changes?

The Aspect of Amputation in the Theatre Space:

S : I want to relate an experience during the production of "TOKYO GHETTO" in Zagreb, Croatia. The performance was interrupted twice by a spectator intervening in the performance. I realised that neither the boundary between the stage and seats nor the joining of the two were important. I think the precise moment of that interruption was very important. It was only a few seconds, and happened twice, but a division

appeared at those moment. A man was hitting a woman. Seeing that, the spectator came to the stage from his seat, and pulled the legs out from under him yelling "Stop it!" The actor fell down, and spectators started making a lot of noise. He thought the actor looked back at him angrily, as if to say 'back off!'

But the actor didn't stop, and began hitting her again so some of the spectators started an uproar, calling out "Stop it!" one after another. He got up heroically amidst the noise, and pulled the actor away again. But without looking back the actor started to hit her again. If the audience member repeated it a third time, the situation would have got out of hand, so I was preparing to get up on stage to say "Please continue watching the show until the end", but the scene changed before there was time and the performance succeeded in continuing.

What I mean to say is, maybe he thought the actor would look back at him. I think he went up on stage hoping the actor would look at him. Meaning he met something he didn't expect, another completely different from him. He was exposed to the Other. I think a split appeared there. In other words, a hidden division which cannot usually be

TOKYO GHETTO - ORGIE @ Eurokaz Festival, Croatia (1996)

seen appeared. You could see the dividing line rip the space open between the two men. In this moment the essence of their bodies normally confined by Image was revealed by accident.

O : To the spectators ?

S : Yes, to everyone.

O : To the spectator who got up as well?

S : Yes, perhaps, it was he who saw it most. After the performance when asked by a German journalist why he intervened in the performance he went on and on about the act. According to the article, he spoke about the couple living next door.
He said he could hear the husband beating his wife every night. He wanted to stop it, but couldn't because he looked far stronger. He said he counted how many times he hit her every night, while she screamed. He said until then he had been a pathetic individual but felt at the theatre that night at long last he had succeeded in stopping violence.

O : What year was that?

S : 1996 at the Eurokaz Festival. It was an international theatre festival which specially focused on theatre at the forefront of the next generation. That experience had such a big a impact on me.
It would be easy to say Theatre of Images has changed to "Theatre of Body", but it wouldn't be true. To be precise, Theatre of Images is amputated by meaning or by accident. That momentary division has

revealed that the body is confined and unable to express. At the site of amputation of the Theatre of Images, the formation of "Theatre of Body" can be seen.

Away from Drama and Community:

O : You came across this by accident. But, it was in your sub-conscious wasn't it? Up until that time you weren't aware of it, but you recognised the division by the accident, didn't you?
Listening to you I remember Kantor wrote about the dividing line. While known as the theatre death, he wanted to engage with people outside the existent cultural or religious bodies. People who have been exiled are destined to have various experiences, and by accepting their destiny, they who were 'disappeared' return. When he or she returns to a community, while he or she may seem ordinary, they aren't. They remain on the doorstep of the community, preferring to stand and look in from there. Its a very strange scene but in his opinion performers have always been such people, since their origins. Their faces and shape are the same as ordinary people, but they are far from being like us, they have a different nature. Kantor wrote this in his manifesto "Theater of Death"; "It is necessary to recover the primeval force of the shock taking place at the moment when opposite a man (the viewer) there stood for the first time, a man (the actor) deceptively similar to us yet at the same time infinitely foreign, beyond an impassable barrier."
In this moment we have a terrible sense of foreboding, fearfully expecting to see the birth of a new strain of human. Kantor

believed this was what theatre was for. When examining exactly what happens at such a moment - as I have wanted to change our discussion to focus on the purpose of audience - the audience are able through discovery to glimpse an opportunity to transform. I agree with him. With this in mind, existence in the world of the performer must be completely different from existence here, and they must be abject. That is the structural nature of theatre.

It becomes apparent from what you have said, although not knowing of Kantor's philosophy of "Theatre of Death" you are saying the same thing. Many people think theatre is primarily based on sympathy because since ancient Greek drama the affinitive relationship between audience and performance has always been regarded as important. That's why people believe ancient theatres in Greece were round.

S : Yes, it is often said so.

O : And in the case of modern theatres, there is a stage slightly above the seats, which are like a bed for catfish. So, when someone says "let's make a round theatre outdoors in order to get rid of such flat atmosphere...

S : (laughing) Yes.

O : But that is far from the nature of theatre. This talk has nothing whatsoever to do with theatre. So, it is the dramatic event which incidentally becomes clearer by this kind of accident. And this event enables us to recognise the essential theatrical structure.

Finally, please tell what you're concerned with now.

Bodies of War and Phantom Pain:

S : Bodies of War. Bodies to be produced for wars of the future, bodies discovered through past wars. The former is related with the aforementioned "Theatre of Body", which will enable us to see past. As a technique, it is similar to physical movement, but in my image it means an uncontrollable "crowd", a crowd which disappears in the light. These are the dead bodies of Iraqi soldiers, you could call them the dead army. Anyway, I want to reveal the various dividing lines between the classes of South and North. The latter is what I call "neuro-system" or the state of "phantom pain". It can be compared to a loss of body perception due to amputation, a kind of virtual actuality.

O : Like the pain you feel in a lost leg?

S : Yes, it is an illusion. The movement of a leg torn off, the sensation of the limbless living body, are shown in our system of "senses" and "atmosphere". I want to clearly specify what these things are in a body system. So I'm running with this process.

O : How have you come to do this?

S : In 1998, most of the membership changed, and the new young members were neither actors or actresses nor dancers. They had no intention of becoming so. As it is difficult to categorise accurately, maybe they can just be called bodies. It is so important for me to be able to confront such bodies which are starting from scratch, uninformed by process.

To summarise, I want to say that the "Theatre of Body" includes crisis within its structure: a crisis that is recollected in "Theatre of Images". If amputation is unsuccessful, many spectators will be satisfied and immediately consume the image. It's like walking a tightrope.

It is said that the bodies I present are very real. But, this is a fallacy, real bodies do not, they cannot exist. Like I said before, we live within the result, within the system, so we don't exist, we only experience our bodies. This basically is impossible to discuss. The so-called real as used to oppose the virtual is merely part of an overall 'image language'. In this way paradoxically, it prevails all over the world at once. By contrast, that is far removed from what I am doing. I use abject materials such as sweat, blood, and pain, not because they are real but because they are virtual. Virtual things are more important. How can we perceive our arms, legs, bodies as specks on the planet? This actuality is an urgent problem in the progress of media technology. Secondly, in the beginning I thought a lot about cloned bodies. The more advanced clone technology, the less power nations have, as they make nations redundant. This is because control and production of labour for which capitalism has always depended on nations, would become possible with no government interference. Capitalism could produce labour independently, which is unacceptable to nations. So, as globalization advances, the existence of the human clone offers a moral ambivalence which is unsolvable.

Just now I was saying new members were just bodies. I saw an opportunity in them to represent the human clone. For example to present bodies as inorganic substances which have lost the tension of living. These bodies don't see this world. They are just shown scenes on the surface of their eyes. For example, is it possible to express the clone through the physical quality of a mineral substance? At present I haven't been able to find a way, but I'm trying. Anyway, I find it so important to recognise that our bodies are not in our possession yet. Lastly I want to make war bodies historical. At the risk of making a foregone conclusion, I will make the connection between these bodies and 'shell-shocked' bodies which appeared first after World War I. Moreover, they were 'bodies in deep trenches'. It is the syndrome Freud discovered, where soldiers after months at the front hide in deep trenches.

In autumn, we're going to perform around Europe and the States for almost three months. Those bodies uncovered in the beginning of the 20th century will be rediscovered at the beginning of this century. I want to converse with audiences from all over the world through these performances.

Shimizu Shinjin
(Artistic Director of Gekidan KAITAISHA)

Otori Hidenaga
(Theatre Critic)

KAITAISHA Biography

劇団解体社　上演データ

The Drifting View
遊行の景色

August 25, 1985
@ Hinoemata Performance Festival ／ヒノエ
マタ・パフォーマンス・フェスティバル

Shimizu: As if trying to make us understand
that it is indeed a perceivable substance, the
wind fills, expands, flutters, and turns inside
out. And it is expected to have a form by
means of mediums.

Onobu: In fact, the body <medium> lets the
wind through, lets it blow through without
demanding any form. Besides, the body itself
is a transformation device that twists the wind
and changes its quality. You see, we are like
bells that ring in a puff of breeze.

—— From "Conversation with no catalyst"

清水　現前たる物質であるということを識らせ
ようとでもするように、風は、孕み、膨らみ、
翻り、裏返る。そして媒体によって形式を求め
られる。
大信　つまり身体〈媒体〉は、風を通すという
こと、形式を求めずに通してしまうということ。
また、身体自体が、風を曲げ、変質させる変換
装置であるんだ。フッとそよいだ風に鳴る鈴で
すよ、我々は。
——「触発人のいない会話」より

Mitsurin-tan
密林譚

January 18-19, 25-26, February 1-2, 1986
@ Yokohama National University dormito-
ries ／横浜国立大学鎌倉蒼翠寮
Artistic Director : Shimizu Shinjin, Onobu
Noriaki
構成・演出　清水信次、大信典明
Cast : Haginaka Minoru, Matsunaka Seiji,
Matsunaga Toru, Kumagai Yuko, Hasegawa
Kazuhiro
出演　萩中稔、松中聖治、松永徹、熊谷裕子、
長谷川和弘

The Drifting View II
遊行の景色 II

August 23-25, 1986
@ Hinoemata Performance Festival ／ヒノエ
マタ・パフォーマンス・フェスティバル

DEAR, SPECTRUM

December 20-21, 27-28, 1986
January 10-11, 17-18, 1987
@ Alternative Art Space - Ofuna monorail
station ／オルターナティブ・アート・スペー
ス・モノレール大船駅
Artistic Director : Shimizu Shinjin
演出　清水信臣
Cast : Onobu Noriaki, Hino Hiruko,
Haginaka Minoru, Kumamoto Kenjiro,
Yamamoto Tetsuya, Isobe Kenichi
出演　大信典明、日野昼子、萩中稔、熊本賢治
郎、山本哲也、磯部健一

'TIS A NIGHT LIKE THE
THEATRICAL P-TIME

July 10-12, 1987
@ Baus Theatre, Kichijoji, Tokyo ／吉祥寺バ

ウスシアター
Artistic Director : Shimizu Shinjin
作・構成・演出　清水信臣
Cast : Onobu Noriaki, Haginaka Minoru,
Hasegawa Kazuhiro, Kumamoto Kenjiro,
Yamamoto Tetsuya, Kaida Genji, Morinaga
Junko, Okada Aya, Hino Hiruko
出演　大信典明、萩中稔、長谷川和弘、熊本賢
治郎、山本哲也、海田玄二、森永純子、岡田綾、
日野昼子
Music : Isobe Kenichi
音楽　磯部健一
Photo : Ishikawa Toshiaki
写真　石川利明
Film & E.Bass : Nishimura Takuya
フィルム・ E.Bass　西村卓也

It has been a long time since we last performed in a theatre, but what we are presenting this time is not a play. I think that the
mere reproduction of a story no longer has
any impact nowadays. TV dramas are
enough for that.
The "theatre" that we create will be re-estab-
lished as an open museum that conveys the
dream of integrating different forms of
expression to people of the present age. All
the seats are <covered>. Please choose
another place you like and see our performance.
Shimizu Shinjin
— From "Future of the Theatre"

　久しぶりに劇場で上演することになったが、
今回提出する舞台は芝居ではない。物語の単純
な再現などもはやこの都市にはいかなるインパ
クトも与えることはできないだろう。テレビド
ラマで充分だ。
　我々の創造する「劇場」は、表現の総合の夢
を現代に伝える開かれた美術館として復活する
ことだろう。観客席はすべて〈梱包〉してある。
どうかお好きな場所で見物していただきたいと
思う。
清水信臣
—「劇場の未来」より

The Drifting View III - White Night
遊行の景色 III －白夜－

September 5, 1987
@ Hinoemata Performance Festival ／ヒノエ
マタ・パフォーマンス・フェスティバル

Bo-Home- Home Wandering
Bo-Home －さまよえる家－

January 8, 15, 22, 29, 1989
@ Around Atelier "Kenzo-sha"／ Moving
Theater 解体社アトリエ「犬蔵舎」一帯
Artistic Director : Shimizu Shinjin
作・構成・演出　清水信臣
Cast : Onobu Noriaki, Haginaka Minoru,
Hino Hiruko, Kumamoto Kenjiro, Hasegawa
Kazuhiro, Isobe Kenichi, Kawakami Takushi,
Takahashi Akinori, Kaida Genji, Maruoka
Hiromi, Nakajima Miyuki, Shibazaki
Tomonori
出演　大信典明、萩中稔、日野昼子、熊本賢治
郎、長谷川和弘、磯部健一、川上琢史、高橋彰
規、海田玄二、丸岡ひろみ、中嶋みゆき、柴崎
智徳
Music : Isobe Kenichi
音楽　磯部健一
Stage Design : Okamoto Isao
舞台美術　岡本功
Lighting Design : Hanada Satoshi
照明　花田智
Installation : Tono Mirai
モニュメント　遠野未来
8mm film : Nishikawa Takuya
8ミリ　西村卓也
35mm slide : Ishikawa Toshiaki
スライド　石川利明

The motif of this work comes from "The
Odyssey".
After having helped lead the Athenians to
victory in the Trojan War, on his way back to
his home country, Ithaca, the protagonist
Odysseus (The King of Ithaca) travels about
on the African coast and the Mediterranean
islands where monsters and witches live. He
drifts about for ten years, having lost his ship
and his men.
"The Odysseia" (Song of Odysseus) is a story
about the circumstances of his drift and the
return back to his country during this period.
"Bo-Home," however, takes this tale of
Odysseus' drift as the essence of its story
development. It dramatizes in pluralistic,

multilateral, and multi-layered approaches the "illusions" of people engaged in "families of today" (the father is the "hero", the mother is the "love", the child is the "future") through interactions with body acting, electronic music, objects and images.
—— From the brochure: "Bo-Home"

　この作品は、ホメロスの作と伝えられる古代ギリシャの長編叙事詩「オデュッセイア」をモチーフにしています。
　主人公オデュッセウス（イタケー王）は、トロイ戦争を勝利に導いた後、故国（イタケー）へ帰国の途上、怪物や魔女の住むアフリカ沿岸や地中海の島々を巡り、船も部下も失い10年のあいだ漂流しました。
　「オデュッセイア」（オデュッセウスの歌）はこの間の漂泊と帰国の事情を描いた物語ですが、「Bo-Home」は、このオデュッセウスの漂流譚をストーリー展開の骨子にして、「現代の家庭」を営む人々の〈幻想〉＝父は「英雄」という／母は「愛」という／子は「未来」という＝を、身体演技と電子音楽、オブジェ、映像とのかかわりの只中から多元的多面的多層的に舞台化したものです。
—— 「Bo-Home」パンフレットより

The Drifting View IV - misty color variation of Odysseia
遊行の景色 IV －霧色に変奏される
オデュッセイア－

August 6, 1989
@ Toga International Arts Festival '89 ／利賀
フェスティバル '89
Artistic Director : Shimizu Shinjin
構成・演出　清水信臣
Cast : Onobu Noriaki, Hino Hiruko, Kumamoto Kenjiro, Nakajima Miyuki, Haginaka Minoru, Isobe Kenichi, Kawakami

Takushi, Takahashi Akinori, Hasegawa Kazuhiro, Maruoka Hiromi
出演　大信典明、日野昼子、熊本賢治郎、中嶋みゆき、萩中稔、磯部健一、川上琢史、高橋彰規、長谷川和弘、丸岡ひろみ
Music : Isobe Kenichi
音楽　磯部健一
Installation : Tono Mirai
建築　遠野未来
Lighting Design : Hanada Satoshi
照明　花田智
8mm film : Nishimura Takuya
８ミリ　西村卓也

During the past few years, we have been performing our works in places like ruins, a station, a garden, a river, or a dam. All of these venues had in them the aspect of "movement," though each were different in scale. (Sometimes, we walked the distance of 10 kilometers with the audience while performing.) To liberate the theatre from being fixed in one place and to throw it out into the whirlpool of more ambiguous relations - "The Drifting View" also means drama in a strange land envisaging the rebirth of "scenery."
Now, "The Odyssey" is used as material for the score development in this piece. With this story of drift as its base, I try to depict images of the departure or return of wandering illusional, itinerant artists. By comparing the square in the performance site to the Mediterranean Sea where Sirens fly, and the riverside street to the Ogygian Island and the House of Circe, and the river to Ithaca, all becomes dramatized and starts to "move". In the midst of <The Drifting View> where the bodies, the images, the objects, and the machine music mingle with each other in multi-layers, I hope to paradoxically explain the reason for this "movement" and our feeling of living in very narrow spaces, that comes from being settled in this "scenery." There are no seats installed. I hope that with the actors, you will also be able to enjoy the "feeling of drift."
Shinjin Simizu
—— From the brochure: "Toga Festival '89"

　この数年、廃墟や駅、庭園、川、ダムなどで作品を上演してきたが、そのどれもがスケールの差はあれ「移動」という事態を伴っていた。（時には観客と共に10キロの行程を演じながら歩いた。）劇を、固定した場所性から解放し、より多義的な関係の渦のなかに投げ出してみること――〈遊行の景色〉とは「風景」の新生を目論む異郷の演劇の謂でもある。
　さて今スコアは「オデュッセイア」を展開の素材にしている。この漂流譚を下敷きに、流浪する幻想の旅芸人たちの出発、あるいは帰還の

イメージを重ねて描いた。会場内の「広場」は
セイレンが翔びかう地中海に、川沿いの「道路」
はオーギュギエ島とキルケの館、「川」はイタ
ケーという〈見立て〉で劇化され「移動」して
行く。身体、映像、オブジェ、マシン音楽が多
層的に交錯する〈遊行の景色〉のただなかで、
〈移動〉の理由を、「風景」に定住する私たちの
〈狭生感〉を、逆説的に提出できればと思う。
「客席」は設置していない。演者共々「漂流感
覚」を楽しんでいただけたらと思っている。
清水信臣
── 「利賀フェスティバル '89」パンフレットより

る。が、あの壮大な物語を上演しようなどとい
うことでは無論ない。ここで提出しているのは、
地獄・煉獄・天国それぞれの、〈イメージの空
間化〉とでもいうような演劇である。切り口は
メディアテックと肉体。現在はこれにつきる。
　今回は室内だけで上演することになった。無
性に俳優の〈肖像〉に出会いたくなったのがそ
の理由である。観客席も固定した。「再定住感
覚」を体験していただけたらと思っている。
清水信臣
── 「JEANNE」パンフレットより

The Drifting View V - T-P
遊行の景色 V − T-P −

August 1989
@ Hinoemata Performance Festival ／ヒノエ
マタ・パフォーマンス・フェスティバル

JEANNE -
Repermanent Residents
JEANNE −再定住者達−

January 25-27, February 1-3, 1991
@ Kenzo-sha, Kawasaki ／犬蔵舎
Artistic Director : Shimizu Shinjin
作・構成・演出　清水信臣
Cast : Hino Hiruko, Haginaka Minoru,
Kumamoto Kenjiro, Nakajima Miyuki,
Maruoka Hiromi, Hasegawa Kazuhiro,
Onobu Noriaki
出演　日野昼子、萩中稔、熊本賢治郎、中嶋み
ゆき、丸岡ひろみ、長谷川和弘、大信典明

Although the source of its development
comes from "The Divine Comedy" by Dante,
it goes without saying that I am not trying to
present the magnificent story itself here.
What I am trying to show is rather a performance as an "image-spatialization" of Hell,
Purgatory and Heaven. Media-technology
and the body are the means of approach,
which are the only possibilities at this
moment.
This time, we will only play indoors. The
reason for this is that I suddenly had an urge
to see the "portraits" of the actors. With the
seats also being fixed, I hope that you will be
able to experience "a feeling of resettlement."
Shimizu Shinjin
── From the brochure: "Jeanne"

展開の素材はダンテの「神曲」に想を得てい

The Drifting View VI -
Shining Heights
遊行の景色 VI −Shining Heights −

August 3-4, 1991
@ Kawaguchi World Festival Fusion '91 ／川
口・エディンバラ World Festival Fusion '91
Artistic Director : Shimizu Shinjin
作・構成・演出　清水信臣
Cast : Hino Hiruko, Haginaka Minoru,
Kumamoto Kenjiro, Nakajima Miyuki,
Maruoka Hiromi, Saito Masako, Hasegawa
Kazuhiro, Kaida Genji, Iida Koji, Narui
Terumitsu, Onobu Noriaki
出演　日野昼子、萩中稔、熊本賢治郎、中嶋み
ゆき、丸岡ひろみ、さいとうまさこ、長谷川和
弘、海田玄二、飯田幸司、成井輝光、大信典明

遊行の景色　by 解体社

THE DOG I -
People in a foreign land
THE DOG I －異郷の子ら－

July 24-25, 30-31, August 1, 6-8, 1993
@ Hongo DOK, Tokyo ／本郷 DOK
Artistic Director : Shimizu Shinjin
作・構成・演出　清水信臣
Cast : Kumamoto Kenjiro, Hino Hiruko, Nakajima Miyuki, Maruoka Hiromi, Kosugi Yoshiko, Moriyama Masako, Takada Miho, Nomoto Ryoko, Ueda Yumiko, Yamagata Mitsuko, Haginaka Minoru, Iida Koji, Kaida Genji, Hasegawa Kazuhiro, Onobu Noriaki
出演　熊本賢治郎、日野昼子、中嶋みゆき、丸岡ひろみ、小杉佳子、森山雅子、高田美穂、野元良子、上田由美子、山形美津子、萩中稔、飯田幸司、海田玄二、長谷川和弘、大信典明
Music : Narui Terumitsu
音楽　成井輝光

Racial and tribal conflicts are overwhelming, famines are disastrous, refugees are overflowing; all are triggered by the end of the Cold War. The world now most resembles a piece of glass which has been completely shattered. What is asked of us as avant-garde theatre artists is to formulate a radically innovative acting theory, corresponding to our post-colonial sense of the world. Actors are raw materials who have to live through the aphoria of the age, in the midst of the exposed impossibilities of human relations. In the latter half of the 80s we started to tackle this issue, by choosing the site of our performance in outdoor spaces, (in railway stations, in parks, and on the road). Our experimental quest for a new acting style continued after we had settled ourselves in a small indoor space at Hongo, Tokyo. It came to a creative formulation in our acting styles, some of which are called "Sculptural Postures," "Walking Postures," and "Fighting Postures."
These are styles in which truly personal and independent "existential gestures" are distilled from actors' social and seemingly individual bodies; that body which is ordained to surrender to its environment, which is kept under surveillance, and which is suppressed by its own history. These gestures are a body-in-motion, "a glory of autonomy" for life-sized individual actors, which can stand against the collective violence and cruelty, observed and experienced all over the world today.
Shimizu Shinjin
── From "THE DOG" Director's note

民族紛争、少数部族の対立、飢餓の増大、難民の流出、冷戦後の世界はまるで粉々に砕け散った鏡のようです。現在、演劇の前衛に求められているものは、まさにこの「ポスト植民地時代」に対応する新たな演技論の構築であるかと思います。俳優という存在こそ、この時代のアポリアを、剥き出しの「関係性」のただなかで生きざるをえない生々しい実態だからです。
私たちは80年代後半から、野外空間を公演場所に選び、駅や公園また路上などでの上演を通してこの課題に取り組み始めました。それら野外での実践的模索は、93年、東京本郷の小空間に拠点を移した後も継続して探求され、「彫像態」「歩行態」「闘技態」などと名付けられた独自の演技様式として結実したのです。端的にいえばそれらは、それぞれの俳優が個人的に負っている肉体―風土に屈し、街に監視され、生活史に抑圧された結果としての肉体―から、俳優各人の真に固有の〈実存的身振り〉を抽出したものであるといえるかと思います。それはまた、群れて勇ましい現代のもろもろの世界観に対抗する等身大の俳優の「固体化の栄光」なのだと考えるものです。
清水信臣
──「THE DOG」パンフレットより

【U.S.A. Tour 1993】

The Drifting View VII
- The Last Walk
遊行の景色 VII
－The Last Walk －

September 13-14, 1993
@ Atlanta Arts Festival '93, Piedmont Park, Atlanta ／アトランタ、ピエドモント・パーク
（アトランタ・アーツ・フェスティバル '93)

THE DOG I -
People in a foreign land
THE DOG I －異郷の子ら－

September 19-20, 1993
@ Park Elevator, Charlotte N.C., U.S.A.／
シャーロット、パークエレベーター
Artistic Director : Shimizu Shinjin
作・構成・演出　清水信臣
Cast : Onobu Noriaki, Haginaka Minoru, Hino Hiruko, Kumamoto Kenjiro, Nakajima Miyuki, Maruoka Hiromi, Iida Koji, Moriyama Masako, Kosugi Yoshiko, Takata Miho, Nomoto Ryoko, Ueda Yumiko, Yamagata Mitsuko
出演　大信典明、萩中稔、日野昼子、熊本賢治郎、中嶋みゆき、丸岡ひろみ、飯田幸司、森山雅子、小杉佳子、高田美穂、野元良子、上田由美子、山形美津子、長谷川和弘
Music : Narui Terumitsu
音楽　成井輝光
Producer : Aoki Michiko(P.A.T.)
制作　青木道子（P.A.T.）

1994

[Trilogy THE DOG ／ THE DOG 三部作]

THE DOG I -
People in a foreign land
THE DOG I －異郷の子ら－

May 13-15, 20-22, 1994

THE DOG II - A Little Story

June 3-5, 10-12, 17-19, 1994

THE DOG III - Saint Orgie
THE DOG III －聖オルギアー

July 1-3, 8-10, 15-17, 1994

@ Hongo DOK, Tokyo ／本郷 DOK
Artistic Director : Shimizu Shinjin
作・構成・演出　清水信臣
Cast : Hino Hiruko, Kumamoto Kenjiro, Nakajima Miyuki, Maruoka Hiromi, Kosugi Yoshiko, Moriyama Masako, Takata Miho, Nomoto Ryoko, Yamagata Mitsuko, Iida Koji, Kaida Genji
出演　日野昼子、熊本賢治郎、中嶋みゆき、丸岡ひろみ、小杉佳子、森山雅子、高田美穂、野

元良子、山形美津子、飯田幸司、海田玄二
Music : Narui Terumitsu
音楽　成井輝光
Company Manager : Maruoka Hiromi
制作　丸岡ひろみ

TRIROGY
THE DOG
PEOPLE IN
A FOREIGN LAND
(U.S.A.VERSION)
A LITTLE STORY
(THE LAST WALK
INDOOR VERSION)
SAINT ORGIE

1995

TOKYO GHETTO -
Voidness has gone, and the era of absurdity is coming.
TOKYO GHETTO －空虚は去り、愚劣の時代がやってくる－

February 25-26, March 3-5, 10-12, 1995
@ Hongo DOK, Tokyo ／本郷 DOK
Artistic Director : Shimizu Shinjin
Cast : Hino Hiruko, Kumamoto Kenjiro, Nakajima Miyuki, Maruoka Hiromi, Kosugi Yoshiko, Moriyama Masako, Takata Miho, Nomoto Ryoko, Yamagata Mitsuko, Iida Koji
出演　日野昼子、熊本賢治郎、中嶋みゆき、丸岡ひろみ、小杉佳子、森山雅子、高田美穂、野元良子、山形美津子、飯田幸司
Lighting Design : Hasegawa Kazuhiro
照明　長谷川和弘
Sound & Visual effects : Hata Takeshi
音響・映像　秦岳志
Company Manager : Maruoka Hiromi
制作　丸岡ひろみ

The Drifting View VIII - They have no name
遊行の景色 VIII
－彼女らに名前はない－

May 1995
@ Toga International Arts Festival '95 ／利賀
新緑フェスティバル '95

The Proscenium - TOKYO GHETTO

September 13-14, 1995
@ Tokyo International Festival of Performing Arts '97, Tokyo Metropolitan Art Space ／東京芸術劇場中ホール（東京国際舞台芸術フェスティバル'95)
Artistic Director : Shimizu Shinjin
作・構成・演出　清水信臣
Cast : Hino Hiruko, Kumamoto Kenjiro, Nakajima Miyuki, Maruoka Hiromi, Iida Koji, Kosugi Yoshiko, Moriyama Masako, Takata Miho, Nomoto Ryoko, Yamagata Mitsuko
出演　日野昼子、熊本賢治郎、中嶋みゆき、丸岡ひろみ、飯田幸司、小杉佳子、森山雅子、高田美穂、野元良子、山形美津子
Lighting Design : Kawai Naoki
照明　河合直樹
Visual Effects : Hata Takeshi
映像　秦岳志
Company Manager : Maruoka Hiromi
制作　丸岡ひろみ

TOKYO GHETTO - ORGIE
TOKYO GHETTO －オルギア－

September 21-24, 1995
@ Shitamachi Theatre Festival '95 ／浅草フランス座（下町演劇祭'95)
Artistic Director : Shimizu Shinjin
作・構成・演出　清水信臣
Cast : Hino Hiruko, Kumamoto Kenjiro, Nakajima Miyuki, Maruoka Hiromi, Iida Koji, Kosugi Yoshiko, Moriyama Masako, Takata Miho, Nomoto Ryoko, Yamagata Mitsuko
出演　日野昼子、熊本賢治郎、中嶋みゆき、丸岡ひろみ、飯田幸司、小杉佳子、森山雅子、高田美穂、野元良子、山形美津子
Company Manager : Maruoka Hiromi
制作　丸岡ひろみ

TOKYO GHETTO III - Dying Anarchy
TOKYO GHETTO III
－瀕死のアナーキー－

March 1-3, 8-10, 15-17, 23-24, 29-31, 1996
@ Hongo DOK, Tokyo ／本郷 DOK
Artistic Director : Shimizu Shinjin
作・構成・演出　清水信臣
Cast : Hino Hiruko, Kumamoto Kenjiro, Nakajima Miyuki, Maruoka Hiromi, Iida Koji, Kosugi Yoshiko, Moriyama Masako, Nomoto Ryoko, Takata Miho, Yamagata Mitsuko,
出演　日野昼子、熊本賢治郎、中嶋みゆき、丸岡ひろみ、飯田幸司、小杉佳子、森山雅子、野元良子、高田美穂、山形美津子
Company Manager : Maruoka Hiromi
制作　丸岡ひろみ

【Croatia Tour 1996】

TOKYO GHETTO - Lullaby

June 26, 1996
@ Kino Ivancica, Zlatar Bistrica, Croatia ／

TOKYO GHETTO - Orgie

June 29-30, 1996
@ Eurokaz Festival '96, Kerempuh Theatre,
Zagreb, Croatia ／クロアチア・ザグレブ、
Kerempuh 劇場（ユーロカズ・フェスティバル
'96）

TOKYO GHETTO - L'épuisé
TOKYO GHETTO －消尽－

July 3, 1996
@ Pulsky Festival, INK, Pula, Croatia ／クロ
アチア・プーラ、INK（Pulsky フェスティバ
ル '96）

Everyone that you see in our productions has
been excluded from, and cast out of society.
They are people who have been erased from
history by the Establishment, and who will be
effaced from civilisation. In effect, they are
'women,' 'children,' 'animals' and the war-
renouncing Constitution of Japan.
The world of our theatre is a lightless world
under representation. "The crisis of representation" is going on quietly, deep within the
countries committing or committed to democ-
racy. And under that, the lightless world
spreads out without limits. To be exact, it is a
barren region; the ruins of the world of "the
body" itself, which is exposed to all manner
of violence.
I put these concepts on stage. When I work
on a production, the first thing I do is to res-
cue these concepts from the tedious discourse
of alienation. I have to find a directing
method that cynicism cannot assimilate. I
work on a production using a method which I
call "sur-documentalism". Basically, this
means more than crafting the skill to con-
struct or edit the facts. It aims to present a
vision and passion about creation that fires
each performer to have the will to live.
Shimizu Shinjin
── From "Croatia Tour 1996" Director's
Message

　我々の劇の登場人物は、皆、体制から排除され
た者たちである。
　歴史から消され、文明に抹殺されようとして
いる者たちである。
　この者たち－それは現実には「女性」、「子供」、
「動物」そして日本国の平和憲法である。

　我々の劇世界は、表象の下に広がる光りなき世
界である。
　民主主義諸国家の内部で深く静かに進行して
いる「表象の危機」。まさにその足下から果てし
なく広がっている光りなき世界である。端的にそこは
不毛の領域である。ありとあらゆる暴力に晒さ
れた－「身体」それ自体－の廃墟である。

　私はこれらの事柄を舞台化する。舞台化するに
あたっては、なによりもまずこれらの事柄をあ
りふれた疎外論から救い出さねばならない。シ
ニシズムに回収されない演出方法が発明されね
ばならない。私は、私が＜シュルドキュメンタリ
ズム＞と名付けた手法を用いて舞台化を行う。
一言でいえばそれはたんに事実を構成／編集す
る技術であることを超えて、役者一人一人に
「生への勇気」を指し示す創作理念たらんとする
ものである。
清水信臣
──「クロアチア・ツアー'96」パンフレットより

TOKYO GHETTO - HARD CORE
TOKYO GHETTO －ハード・コアー

December 19-23, 1996
@ Japan Foundation Forum, Tokyo ／国際交
流フォーラム
Artistic Director : Shimizu Shinjin
作・構成・演出　清水信臣
Cast : Kumamoto Kenjiro, Hino Hiruko,
Nakajima Miyuki, Maruoka Hiromi, Kosugi
Yoshiko, Iida Koji, Moriyama Masako,
Nomoto Ryoko, Hagiwara Michihide, Takata
Miho, Yamagata Mitsuko
出演　熊本賢治郎、日野昼子、中嶋みゆき、丸
岡ひろみ、小杉佳子、飯田幸司、森山雅子、野
元良子、萩原道英、高田美穂、山形美津子
Lighting Design : Hasegawa Kazuhiro
照明　長谷川和弘
Sound & Visual effects : Hata Takeshi
音響・映像　秦岳志

Company Manager : Maruoka Hiromi
制作　丸岡ひろみ

【Europe Tour 1997】

TOKYO GHETTO - Secret Ceremony
TOKYO GHETTO －密儀－

June 7-8, 1997
@ CCA, Glasgow, Scotland ／スコットラン
ド・グラスゴー、CCA

TOKYO GHETTO - Class in Twilight
TOKYO GHETTO －薄明の階級－

June 13-15, 1997
@ Chapter Arts Centre, Cardiff, Wales ／
ウェールズ・カーディフ、チャプター・アー
ト・センター

TOKYO GHETTO - Orgie#2

June 20-21, 1997
@ Arnolfini, Bristol, England ／イギリス・ブ
リストル、アーノルフィニ

S.M.3F - Tokyo Discipline

June 24-25, 1997
@ Eurokaz Festival '97, Kerempuh Theatre,
Zagreb, Croatia ／ザグレブ、Kerempuh 劇場
（ユーロカズ・フェスティバル'97）

TOKYO GHETTO - Orgie#3

June 27, 1997
@ Zadar Snova '97, Zadar, Croatia ／クロア
チア・ザダル（ザダル・スノーヴァ'97）

TOKYO GHETTO - Orgie#4

July 1, 1997
@ Balance Festival '97, Marburg,
Germany ／ドイツ・マールブルグ（バラン
ス・フェスティバル'97）

【Korea Tour 1997】
The Proscenium - TOKYO GHETTO

September 9-12, 1997
@ Theatre of Nations '97, Munye Theater,
Seoul ／ソウル・文藝会館（シアター・オブ・
ネイションズ'97）

ZERO CATEGORY
零カテゴリー

October 20-26, 1997
@ Tokyo Metropolitan Art Space ／東京芸術

劇場小ホール（東京国際舞台芸術フェスティバ
ル'97）
Artistic Director : Shimizu Shinjin
作・構成・演出　清水信臣
Cast : Hino Hiruko, Kumamoto Kenjiro,
Nakajima Miyuki, Kosugi Yoshiko,
Moriyama Masako, Nomoto Ryoko, Takata
Miho, Yamagata Mitsuko, Ichikawa Aiko,
Hasegawa Tomoko, Urasoe Hisafumi
出演　日野昼子、熊本賢治郎、中嶋みゆき、小
杉佳子、森山雅子、野元良子、高田美穂、山形
美津子、市川愛子、長谷川知子、浦添尚文
Stage Manager : Mitsu Hisashi
舞台監督　三津久
Technical Manager : Hata Takeshi
技術　秦岳志
Lighting Design : Kawai Naoki
照明　河合直樹
Sound : Mizutani Yuji
音響　水谷雄治
Company Manager : Maruoka Hiromi
制作　丸岡ひろみ

The theme of this work is to present on stage
the human "body" as a "representation of
hope" connected to the future. In order to
realize this, two methodological approaches
are tried on the stage. One is the creation of a
new type of primitivism. We, for example,
have forgotten a lot of "the-very-beginnings"
which eanabled us to become the "human
being." Thus, I would like to try to recuperate
them from inside the individual actors; to
excavate the unnameable attraction of the
"body". It might as well be the technique of
transfiguration into something other than a
human being such as an animal or a plant -
and to "dramatize" it on the stage. The other
approach is to attempt to restore communica-
tion in the use of media-technology. In this
work, the actors operate the Internet, mobile
phones, or Polaroid cameras, in actual reality,
that is to say, as an improvisation of "now
and here". Dialogues of "each time" appear
indeed as a repetition of the unrepeatable.
Into this we put our earnest wish to not let the
truth of globalization be empty - the globalization that will probably further accelerate
and evolve in the future.
Shimizu Shinjin
── From the brochure: "Zero Category"

　この作品のテーマは、人間の「身体」を、未
来に繋がる希望の表象として舞台上に提出する
ことです。そのために舞台では二つの方法的ア
プローチが試みられています。ひとつは新たな
プリミティヴィズムの創造です。例えば、私た
ちは「人間」に成る為にさまざまな「原初」を
忘却してきました。それらを俳優の個体の内か
ら救い上げること、名指すことのできぬ「身体」

1998

の魅力─あるいはそれは動物、植物、など人間
以外のものへのトランスフィギュレーションの
技術なのかも知れない─を発掘し、それらを舞
台場に「ドラマ化」することです。もう一つは
メディアテクノロジーを使用したコミュニケー
ション回復へのチャレンジです。この舞台では
インターネット、携帯電話、ポラロイドカメラ
などのオペレーティングが俳優たちの手によ
り、すべて現実に、すなわち「いま、ここ」の
インプロヴィゼーションとして展開されます。
まさに〈その都度〉の対話が、二度と繰り返せ
ない反復として出現します。それは今後ますま
す加速し進化していくであろうグローバリゼー
ションの内実を空疎化してはならないという私
たちの切実な思いが込められているのです。
清水信臣
──「ZERO CATEGORY」パンフレットより

ZERO CATEGORY II -
The Season of New Abjection
零カテゴリー II
─ The Season of New Abjection ─

August 1-3, 1998
@ Art Sphere, Tennoz Isle, Tokyo ／アートス
フィア（天王洲アイル）
Artistic Director : Shimizu Shinjin
作・構成・演出　清水信臣
Cast : Hino Hiruko, Kumamoto Kenjiro,
Nakajima Miyuki, Moriyama Masako,
Nomoto Ryoko, Yamagata Mitsuko, Takata
Miho, Hasegawa Tomoko, Urasoe Hisafumi,
Koike Shunji
出演　日野昼子、熊本賢治郎、中嶋みゆき、森
山雅子、野元良子、山形美津子、高田美穂、長
谷川知子、浦添尚文、小池俊二
Singer : SUEKICHI
歌手　SUEKICHI
Stage Manager : Mitsu Hisashi
舞台監督　三津久

Technical Manager : Hata Takeshi
技術監督　秦岳志
Lighting Design : Kawai Naoki
照明　河合直樹
Sound : Mizutani Yuji
音響　水谷雄治
Company Manager : Kurihara Mayumi
制作　栗原まゆみ

Performance Concept
"Body" as the world - can presently be roughly categorized as follows:

1)New "monstrous bodies" created by the machine and human "nervous system," so to speak, as if the hyper-mega-terminal and our human brain were directly connected and transfigured into "non-human."

2)"Discipligy of control", reacting against the "chaos" interwoven by those numerous bodies.

3)Borderless, "refugee-like bodies" standing motionless, excluded from 1 and 2. Some of these critical bodies deviated from every kind of state programs will soon be included into capital as the means of the lower work force and will thus be reconstructed.

4)Lastly, "abandoned bodies" ; those who are hidden in a psychiatric ward, a prison, or a bedroom, "disgraced."

In this work, I would like to present the manifold power of these "world=bodies."　I hope that we can come to have a variety of "dialogues" with all the audience who are here to attend the performance.
Shimizu Shinjin
—— From the brochure: "ZERO CATEGORY II"

パフォーマンス・コンセプト
「身体」の世界性―それはいま、およそ以下の
カテゴリーに分類されうるだろう。

1)電脳都市と、我々人間の脳髄が直接的に繋がり、〈人間ではないもの〉に変容してゆくような、いわば機械と人間の「神経系」が生み出す新たな「怪物的身体」。

2)それら諸身体の織り成す「無秩序」に対する反動から、統制理念によって再構築されてゆく「規律的身体」。

3)1と2から排除され、茫然と立ち尽くしているボーダーレスな「難民的身体」。あらゆる国家プログラムから逸脱してしまったこの危機的身体のいくつかは、やがて下層労働力として資本に組み込まれ再構成される。

4)最後に「見放された身体」。すなわち「汚辱」として精神病棟、監獄、寝室等に隠されているそれ。

私は、この舞台でこれら「世界＝身体」の諸力を現わしたい。そして劇に立ち会ってくれた観客の皆さんと様々な「対話」が生まれることを願っています。
清水信臣
——「ZERO CATEGORY II」パンフレットより

DE-CONTROL I - Cluster/Act in the Cell
DE-CONTROL I
－群れ／独房アクト－

January 22-24, 28-30, 1999

DE-CONTROL II - Neuro System
DE-CONTROL II － Neuro系－

February 19-21, 25-27, 1999

@ Free Space CANVAS, Tokyo ／ Free Space カンバス
Artistic Director : Shimizu Shinjin
作・構成・演出　清水信臣
Cast : Hino Hiruko, Kumamoto Kenjiro, Nakajima Miyuki, Nomoto Ryoko, Yamagata

Mitsuko, Takata Miho, Hasegawa Tomoko, Urasoe Hisafumi, Koike Shunji, Aota Reiko, Tsuchimoto Tadashi
出演　日野昼子、熊本賢治郎、中嶋みゆき、森山雅子、野元良子、山形美津子、高田美穂、長谷川知子、浦添尚文、小池俊二、青田玲子、圡本正
Company Manager : Kurihara Mayumi
制作　栗原まゆみ

Bye-Bye : Into the Century of Degeneration
バイバイ　－退化の世紀へ－

April 9-11, 1999
@ Setagaya Public Theatre, Tokyo ／世田谷パブリックシアター
Artistic Director : Shimizu Shinjin
作・構成・演出　清水信臣
Cast : Hino Hiruko, Kumamoto Kenjiro, Nakajima Miyuki, Moriyama Masako, Nomoto Ryoko, Yamagata Mitsuko, Takata Miho, Hasegawa Tomoko, Urasoe Hisafumi, Koike Shunji, Aota Reiko, Tsuchimoto Tadashi, Tano Hideko
出演　日野昼子、熊本賢治郎、中嶋みゆき、森山雅子、野元良子、山形美津子、高田美穂、長谷川知子、浦添尚文、小池俊二、青田玲子、圡本正、田野日出子
Stage Manager : Mitsu Hisashi
舞台監督　三津久
Technical Manager : Hata Takeshi
技術監督　秦岳志
Lighting Design : Kawai Naoki
照明　河合直樹
Sound : Mizutani Yuji
音響　水谷雄治
Company Manager : Kurihara Mayumi
制作　栗原まゆみ

"I say good-bye to the beauty and fertility. History has resumed." January 17, 1991

Bye-Bye is the culmination of KAITAISHA's stage productions in the 1990s, that dealt with the physical and political aspects of the human body. The work consists of scenes that were reconstructed to document how that decade fell into functional political disorder.
Shimizu Shinjin
—— From the brochure: "Bye-Bye: Into the Century of Degeneration"

さよならだ　美にも豊饒にも
歴史は再開した　1.17.1991
この劇は、解体社がこの 90 年代に発表してきた身体と権力を巡る諸作品の集大成もしくは総決算ともよぶべきものです。私は、彼／彼女ら

のボディ・ポリティクスが機能不全に陥った我らの 90 年代を〈証言〉し「歴史化」する、その可能性に賭けています。メディア・イメージが造りだす表象のアリーナを破砕しつつ—
清水信臣
—— 「バイバイ—退化の世紀へ—」パンフレットより

DE-CONTROL III - Unexpected Living Thing
DE-CONTROL III
－まだ生き物がいたなんて－

September 17-19, 24-26, 1999

DE-CONTROL IV - Iconoclastic Arena
DE-CONTROL IV
－イコノクラスティック・アリーナ－

October 22-24, 29-31, 1999

@ Free Space CANVAS, Tokyo ／ Free Space カンバス
Artistic Director : Shimizu Shinjin
作・構成・演出　清水信臣
Cast : Hino Hiruko, Kumamoto Kenjiro, Nakajima Miyuki, Moriyama Masako, Nomoto Ryoko, Hasegawa Tomoko, Urasoe Hisafumi, Koike Shunji, Aota Reiko, Tsuchimoto Tadashi, Urayama Mariko, Akaiwa Kazumi, Fujishiro Aki
日野昼子、熊本賢治郎、中嶋みゆき、森山雅子、野元良子、長谷川知子、浦添尚文、小池俊二、青田玲子、圡本正、浦山真理子、赤岩和美、藤代アキ
Company Manager : Kurihara Mayumi
制作　栗原まゆみ

[Melbourne Tour 1999]

Bye-Bye : Into the Century of Degeneration
バイバイ －退化の世紀へ－

December 7, 1999
@ Dancehouse, Melbourne ／オーストラリ
ア・メルンボン、ダンスハウス

Kaitaisha × NYID
Intercultural Collaboration Project
Journey to Con-Fusion

劇団解体社（東京）× NYID（メルボルン）
異文化演劇コラボレーション・プロジェクト

混成への旅

December 8-13, 1999
@ the Open Stage, Melbourne ／オーストラ
リア・メルンボン、オープンステージ
Artistic Director : Shimizu Shinjin, David
Pledger
作・構成・演出　清水信臣、デヴィッド・プレ
ジャー
Cast : Kaitaisha=Hino Hiruko, Kumamoto
Kenjiro, Nakajima Miyuki, Moriyama
Masako, Nomoto Ryoko, Urasoe Hisafumi,
Aota Reiko, Tsuchimoto Tadashi, Urayama
Mariko, Akaiwa Kazumi, Fujishiro Aki,
Hasegawa Tomoko
NYID=Katia Molino, Greg Ulfan, Paul
Bongiovanni, Louise Taube, Simon Hall
出演　解体社＝日野昼子、熊本賢治郎、中嶋み
ゆき、森山雅子、野元良子、浦添尚文、小池俊
二、青田玲子、土本正、浦山真理子、赤岩和美、
藤代アキ、長谷川知子　NYID＝カチア・モリ
ノ、グレッグ・ウルファン、ポール・ボンジョ

バンニ、ルイーズ・タウベ、サイモン・ホール
Producer : Hata Takeshi, Peter Eckersall
制作　秦岳志、ピーター・エッカサール

DE-CONTROL

14 December, 1999
@ Courthouse, Melbourne ／オーストラリ
ア・メルボルン、コートハウス

DE-CONTROL V - many many

April 7-9, 14-16, 2000

DE-CONTROL VI - Prisoner of Freedom
DE-CONTROL VI　－自由の虜－

May 12-14, 19-21, 2000

DE-CONTROL VII - S.M.3F.II
DE-CONTROL VII　－続S.M.3F.－

June 16-18, 23-25, 2000

@ Free Space CANVAS, Tokyo ／ Free
Space カンバス
Artistic Director : Shimizu Shinjin
作・構成・演出　清水信臣
Cast : Hino Hiruko, Kumamoto Kenjiro,
Nakajima Miyuki, Nomoto Ryoko, Urasoe
Hisafumi, Aota Reiko, Tsuchimoto Tadashi,

Urayama Mariko, Akaiwa Kazumi, Fujishiro Aki
出演　日野昼子、熊本賢治郎、中嶋みゆき、野元良子、浦添尚文、小池俊二、青田玲子、上本正、浦山真理子、赤岩和美、藤代アキ
Company Manager : Hata Takeshi
制作　秦岳志

【Hong Kong Tour 2000】

The Death Walk

April 28-30, 2000
@ Journey 2000 Festival, Shouson Theatre, Hong Kong Arts Centre ／香港アートセンター（Journey 2000 Festival）

Exile on the Earth

May 1, 2000
@ Journey 2000 Festival, Hong Kong University of Science and Technology ／香港科学技術大学（Journey 2000 Festival）

Kaitaisha × NYID
Intercultural Collaboration Project
Journey to Con-Fusion 2

劇団解体社（東京）× NYID（メルボルン）
異文化演劇コラボレーション・プロジェクト

混成への旅 2

July 1-9, 2000
@ Morishita Studio, Tokyo ／森下スタジオ
Artistic Director : Shimizu Shinjin, David Pledger
作・構成・演出　清水信臣、デヴィッド・プレジャー

Cast : Kaitaisha=Hino Hiruko, Kumamoto Kenjiro, Nakajima Miyuki, Nomoto Ryoko, Urasoe Hisafumi, Aota Reiko, Tsuchimoto Tadashi, Urayama Mariko, Akaiwa Kazumi, Fujishiro Aki, Hasegawa Tomoko, Ishii Yasuji
NYID=Katia Molino, Greg Ulfan, Louise Taube, Simon Hall
出演　解体社=日野昼子、熊本賢治郎、中嶋みゆき、野元良子、浦添尚文、小池俊二、青田玲子、上本正、浦山真理子、赤岩和美、藤代アキ、長谷川知子、石井康二　NYID＝カチア・モリノ、グレッグ・ウルファン、ルイーズ・タウベ、サイモン・ホール
Producer : Hata Takeshi, Peter Eckersall
制作　秦岳志、ピーター・エッカサール

【Berlin Tour 2000】

The Death Walk

August 12, 18, 2000

Exile on the Earth

August 13, 2000
@ Festival of Vision 2000, Haus der Kulturen der Welt, Berlin ／ドイツ・ベルリン、世界文化の家（Festival of Vision 2000）

Bye-Bye: The New Primitive
バイバイ／未開へ

June 15-17, 21-24, 2001
@ Morishita Studio, Tokyo ／森下スタジオ
Artistic Director : Shimizu Shinjin
作・構成・演出　清水信臣
Cast : Hino Hiruko, Kumamoto Kenjiro, Nakajima Miyuki, Nomoto Ryoko, Urasoe Hisafumi, Aota Reiko, Tsuchimoto Tadashi, Akaiwa Kazumi, Ishii Yasuji, Adam Broinowski, Tano Hideko, Fueda Uichiro
出演　日野昼子、熊本賢治郎、中嶋みゆき、野

元良子、浦添尚文、青田玲子、玉本正、赤岩和美、石井康二、アダム・プロノフスキ、田野日出子、笛田宇一郎
Stage Manager : Mitsu Hisashi
舞台監督　三津久
Lighting Design : Kawai Naoki
照明　河合直樹
Sound : Mizutani Yuji
音響　水谷雄治
Company Manager : Hata Takeshi, Enso Kiyomi
制作　秦岳志、延増静美

First Scene / Crowd
"People come together on the street, they gather, they disperse, each one of them achieves individual changes, and then again, they move incessantly, they dash, they become pressure, they attract each other, they get torn off, they come together again, they make pairs, they make lines, sometimes, they transform into an army, they are vomited, or, they are controlled, they are neglected, they flee, they get followed, they stay with in their limits, they lay their bodies in the night streets of threat and consolation..."

Second Scene / Blood and Earth
"In recent years, people have been talking about the collapse of families. However, is this really true? Have families, in which people helped each other, hated each other, and shared their dreams with each other, really disappeared? Through revealing bodies exposed to violence, I would like to show a "bond" that may be united, in an abyss, even if only a little. "

Third Scene / Future of Human Body
Through presenting the peculiar phenomena of "phantom pain" in numerous bodies starting to wriggle in search of already-lost "memories of the body" or of "virtual reality," the arrival of the forthcoming age for "human body" will be searched for with horrifying and yet beautiful images.
(The actual order of the performance may be different.)
—— From the brochure: "Bye-Bye: The New Primitive"

一場／群れ
「路上に集い、かたまり、分散し、それぞれ固有の変化を成し遂げ、また絶えまなく移動し、疾走し、圧力となり、互いに引きつけあい、引き剥がされ、再び集合し、対となり、列となり、ときに軍隊と化し、吐き出され、または管理され、放置され、逃がれ、追われ、限界にいたり、強迫と慰安の夜の路にその身を横たえ・・・」

二場／血と地
「近年、家族の崩壊が叫ばれて久しい、けれどそれは本当か?ときに支えあい、憎しみあい夢をわかちあった、あの家族が本当になくなってしまったのか―暴力に晒された諸身体の露呈を通して、深淵に、なにかわずかでも、つながっているかもしれぬ「絆」を表したい」

三場／人体の未来
もはや失われてしまった「肢体の記憶」を求めて蠢きはじめる諸身体の独異な「幻肢痛」あるいは「バーチャル・アクチュアリティ」の現出を通して、「人間身体」にとっての来るべき時代の到来が、おぞましくも美しいイメージとともに探求されてゆきます。
(実際の上演順と異なる場合があります)

―― 「バイバイ／未開へ」パンフレットより

【World Tour 2001】

Bye-Bye: The New Primitive
バイバイ／未開へ

September 1-3, 2001
@ LAOKOON Festival 2001, Kampnagel, Hamburg ／ドイツ・ハンブルグ、カンプナーゲル（ラオコオン・フェスティバル 2001）

September 14-15, 2001
@ tanzhaus nrw, Dusseldorf, Germany ／ドイツ・デュッセルドルフ、タンツハウス

September 19-23, 2001
@ Mousonturm, Frankfurt, Germany ／ドイツ・フランクフルト、マーゾンターム

October 4-6, 2001
@ Japan Society, New York, U.S.A.／アメリカ・ニューヨーク、ジャパン・ソサエティ

October 10-11, 2001
@ Chapter at Barry Memorial Hall, Cardiff, Wales ／ウェールズ・カーディフ、チャプター・アート・センター（バリー・メモリアル・ホール）

October 18-19, 2001
@ The Green Room, Manchester, England ／
イギリス・マンチェスター、グリーンルーム

October 23-24, 2001
@ Gardner Arts Centre, Brighton, England ／
イギリス・ブライトン、ガードナー・アート・
センター

October 27, 2001
@ Aberystwyth Arts Centre, Aberystwyth,
Wales ／ウェールズ・アベリスウィス、アベリ
スウィス・アート・センター

October 31 - November 3, 2001
@ ICA, London, England ／イギリス・ロンド
ン、ＩＣＡ

November 10-11, 2001
@ St.Donats Arts Centre, Llantwit Major,
Wales ／ウェールズ、セントドナッツ・アー
ト・センター

［対話］
演劇の生成と攻囲される身体
──グローバリゼーションに抗して

鴻英良＋清水信臣

［対話］演劇の生成と攻囲される身体

——グローバリゼーションに抗して

鴻英良 ＋ 清水信臣

写真—宮内勝

第一部

鴻 今日は、演劇という表象の形式を考えるときに、何が問われているかというような、演劇をめぐるある種原理的な話をしたいですね。具体的に表象としてそれが問われるときに、どういう形式が成立しうるのかというような問題を、表現論として話すというのはどうですか。そのためには、まず九〇年代から二〇〇一年の今日までの十年ぐらいの間に、

演劇の足跡がどういう意味を持っていたのかめる。カントール自身も自分の発言をしています。カントール自身も自分ののような自覚がいろいろな作家に起こりはじ

演劇の足跡がどういう意味を持っていたのかめる。

我々に何が見えてきて、何が見えにくくなってきたのかについて話さなければならないでしょう。つまり、演劇をやっている側も、批評する側も、九〇年代に入って何らかの発見をしていた、と私は思っているわけです。

たとえば、ポーランドの演出家タデウシュ・カントール（一九一五—一九九〇）が、一九八八年に、「終わりが近づいてくるにつれて、明らかになってくるものがある」というようなことを、八〇年代の終わりになって、より自覚的に意識するようになるわけです。そのころ、カントールは、七五年に『死の演劇宣言』を書いたときよりも遥かに明瞭に、「死の演劇」が二十世紀の戦争と密接に関係していたのだと意識するようになります。彼の演劇は「アウシュヴィッツ以降芸術は可能か」というアドルノ的な問いに対する応答であったわけですが、八〇年代終わりぐらいに、そのような自覚がいろいろな作家に起こりはじめる。

ところで、清水さんが、演劇的な方法において、いままでとは違った方向を模索しはじめるのが、八四、五年でしたね。

清水　ええ、八五年のヒノエマタ・パフォーマンスフェスティバルから始めた野外移動演劇ですね。「遊行の景色」と名づけた一連の作品からです。

鴻　ヒノエマタの野外で始めたわけですね。いままで密室劇をやっていた演出家が、野原や河原で演劇を試みはじめたのが、八五年ぐらいだったわけですが、それが何を意味するのかということは、よくわからないでやっていた部分も当然あるわけだけど、何回かやった経験もあると同時に、自分の演劇が変わっていったことの意味とかを改めて考えるということも含めて、八〇年代の終わりぐらいから、そこに一種歴史的意識みたいなものが働いていたのだということを、清水さんは自覚しはじめたのではないか、と私は思っています。

九〇年に入って、解体社が外国で公演する機会も増え、日本国内とは違った観客と出会

い、違った空間というもので上演を始めることによって、そこでまた実際的な演劇の変化を経験する。そうした一連の動きのなかで、重要なことなのではないかと、私は思っているわけです。

演出家として、何を考えていたのか、あるいは具体的にどういう問題に直面したのか、何か決定的に重要な経験をしたのか。自分の演出史のなかで、九〇年代というものが何であったのか。二〇〇一年のいま、それをどういうふうに想起するか。それが演劇にとって重要なことなのではないかと、私は思っているわけです。

これらに直接答える形でもいいし、ややすれてもいいんですけど、表現者として、この二十年、あるいは十五年ぐらいをどういうふうに見てきたのか。そして、その辺から、いま何をやろうとしているのかということを含めて、まず話していただけますか……。

イメージの演劇と媒体としての身体

遊行の景色 ＠ヒノエマタ・パフォーマンスフェスティバル（1985）

清水　そうですね、八〇年代ですか。いろいろな記憶が錯綜していて、話があちこち飛ぶかもしれませんが……。

「野外劇」を始めた理由は文字通り、ともかく「外」へ出たかったんですね。当時いわゆる小劇場演劇とよばれる同時代の演劇を客席に座って観るというのがどうにも辛かったというか、悔恨の回想やら共感の渦のなかに巻き込まれて、これらと同じ土俵でやってい

てもどうしようもないと思っ
たんです。なぜかというと我々の演技も、と
くに演技において彼ら小劇場演劇の担い手た
ちのそれと同じようなものでしたから。だっ
たら、我々の演技がよって立つ諸々の条件と
それを成り立たせている上演スタイル自体を
変えてしまうほかない。要するに、自分たち
の「演技」を不可能にさせてしまおうと考え
ました。

普通、野外劇というと野外劇場での上演の
ことだと思うでしょうが、それでは単に劇場
が屋内にあるか屋外にあるかの違いでしかな
い。私の構想した「野外劇」はまったく違う
ものでした。まず観客席も舞台もつくらない。
白昼でもかまわない。観客も役者も上演空間
を移動する。たとえば河原、公園、路上、駅、
廃屋等の周辺一帯を観客とともにさまよいな
がら演劇的な事柄を見せていこうというもの
ですが、まさにこの時期に「身体」の問題に
遭遇したわけです。この広大で自由な拡散的
状況のただなかでは演技することも踊りだす
こともできない、つまり情念の噴出やら等身
大の自然らしさといった従来の演技術はまっ
たく通用しないんですね。そこで援用された
のが「イメージの演劇」と、これを身体論的
に支える「オブジェとしての身体」もしくは
「媒体としての身体」です。

湾岸戦争と美学の終焉

つまり、ある風景なり空間のなかに限りなく
異物としての身体を配置することによって、そ
の身体を通して、通常私たちが見ていた風景な
り空間およびさまざまな構成体がいつもと違っ
て見える。たとえば駅に到着する列車、歩道橋
を行き交う人々の歩み、走り去る車…見慣れて
いるはずの光景が、上演の経過とともに新しく
更新されていくような感じ、そのような「感覚
の変容」の契機として身体を使う。当時はこの
ような手法にとても魅力を感じていまして、こ
れを野外で、しかも移動しながら見せることに
よって、あるいはまたテクノロジー・アートな
ども用いながら、さらに増幅させようと目論ん
でいました。

私のこうした考え方を破産させたのが九一年
に起こった湾岸戦争です。いままでのモチベー
ションのすべてが一挙に色褪せた、まあ破産状
態ですね。そんなわけで、いったん引き籠もっ
て、身体とそれを包囲する権力という問題系に
取り組みました。とはいっても、当時、稽古場
のあった川崎の倉庫でまる二年、公演も打たず
の「歩行」の稽古ばかりしたという
のが実際のところですが（笑）。

鴻　ある意味で、八〇年代のいわばイメージの
演劇的な形で空間を変容させていくような身体
の再配置の方法は美学的だったということなん
ですね。そしてそれが美学的なものだったのだ
と気づくきっかけが、あなたにとって湾岸戦争
だったわけですね。

清水　政治性が薄いということですよね。とい
うか政治性が表に出てくることができない背景
なり支配的な言説があった。たとえば「グロー
バル・ビレッジ」とか、マクルーハン（一九一
一―一九八〇）ですね。均質化した世界でメ
ディア・テクノロジーが人々の欲望を差異化し
ていく。まさにイメージの演劇ですよね。身体、

音楽、美術、多種多様なエスニシティの差異を、「トータルシアター」の概念の内部に収容し、イメージ消費を加速させるために常に新しい美学的配置が志向される。

そのようなことを考えながら九三年以降の「本郷DOK」での一連の上演に繋げていったわけですが。

鴻　なんで湾岸戦争で、そう思うようになったんですか？　つまり、あの時代、九一年の湾岸戦争以外にも、八九年のベルリンの壁の崩壊とか、九三年のサラエボだとか、契機になるものはいくつかあったと思うのですが、「闘争の場」はいくつかあったと思うのですが、「闘争の場の身体」が露出してくる、そういうふうに自覚される瞬間というのが人によって当然違うでしょうけど、それがあなたにとってなぜ湾岸戦争だったのか？　いまマクルーハンという言葉が出てきたのに繋がるのかもしれないけど、なぜ湾岸戦争だったのかということ、その辺はどうなのですか？

劇場は戦場である

清水　基本的に私は、演劇は「戦争」だと

み替える、権力関係として組み替えてゆく作業別に消費されるという意味において劇場は「戦場」なんです。

ところが湾岸戦争には身体がない。身体のない戦場が九〇年代の幕を開けたというのは演劇にとって衝撃ですよ。それが一つ。もう一つは、先程から話しているメディアによる世界化──テレビですよね。ものすごく大量に映像が流されました。もう誰もが彼がそのメディア・イメージのだたなかにまみれていて、もちろん私も、それまで頼りにしていた私だけの直感などとよんでいたものは消し飛んでしまった、というのが実感でした。

鴻　もちろん、それは「闘争の場としての身体」という言葉で接続しながら、常に演劇に関係しているわけだけど、もうちょっと脱線させてしまうと、湾岸戦争はメディア・テクノロジーに操作された戦争であるというイメージもある。あの当時話題になっていたいくつかの文献のなかで、ボードリヤールの、『湾岸戦争は起こらなかった』がありますね。要するに、彼はハイパー・リアルな空間にお

を通して「闘争の場としての身体」を提示して、権力関係として組み替えてゆく作業「戦場」なんです。

思ってるんですよ。まさに人間の身体が無差別に消費されるという意味において劇場は

湾岸戦争が明らかにしたことは、やろうと思えば、そういった欲望の差異化などというものはすべて一元化できるということです。「多様性」などと我々がよんでいたものは、剥き出しの権力が表に出ない限りにおいて肯定されているのであって、それがいったん発動・行使されたときには一挙に情報統制と危機管理でもって世界を同一性に塗り込めることが簡単にできてしまう。逆に言えば、だからこそ「イメージの演劇」は政治化できる可能性があるとも言える。

たとえば、これはあとで話題になるとは思いますが、イメージの演劇で使われる身体は、本来、いかなる目的も持っていないんです。主体が自己実現していくようなビジョンではない。身体は、あくまでも関係生成のための部品であり、媒体です。空間やオブジェ、あるいは単にそこにあるものとの関係性によって押し出されてくる身体性です。この関係自体を政治的に読

ける闘争の形式として、湾岸戦争を捉えている。その方向で思考することがむしろメディアを制覇することになるのですが、そのことによって身体が失われていくというか、隠蔽されていくという構造が湾岸戦争の勝利の形態だったわけです。そのときに、実際には爆弾が落ちていたわけだし、あるいは油田は多国籍軍によって破壊されていた。あのときは完全な報道管制で、たとえば原油で黒まみれになった二匹の水鳥というのを我々は絶え間なく見せられていたのだけど、世界中の人たちは二匹しか見てないのに、あらゆる水鳥は真っ黒であると信じさせられたわけです。そういう操作のなかで、いわば見えなくされていたもの、隠蔽されたものを清水さんは見ていたということです。

そのような作業と、演出家であるということとの関係は、九〇年代の活動にとって、どういう意味を持っていたのかというのが、重要な問題だと思うんですが。さらに、ずらしてしまうと、そういう想像力を表象に接続させていこうとするときに、たとえば美術家であるとか、小説家であるとか、映画監督であるとか、演劇以外の表象の形式に関わるのではなく、ほかならぬ演劇という表象の形式に関わっていこうとすることは何を意味するのか。たとえば湾岸戦争に眼差しを向けることと、「闘争の場としての身体」というものに接近していくこととがどういうふうに関係しているのか。その点、清水さんはどのように考えていますか？

清水　やはりイマジネーション（想像力）ですよね。泥臭いようですが、とにかく想像力をいまいちど鍛え直さないと。画面を通して、あの砂漠に確かに隠されている、生き埋めにされているイラク兵の死体があるんです。それがいったい、どのような身体なのか、つまり、いかなる意味を持たされた死体なのか、ということに思いを馳せざるをえないわけです。どうしても私は身体にいくんですね。もちろん水鳥もなんですが、やはり身体、人間の身体です。

演劇史との関連で言えば、モダニズム以降、身体が何かの誰かのキャラクターを表現する器であることをやめて、フィジカルなものに──速度や線、角度、重量等に身体を還元していく。データ化していく。そのような果てに人間身体というものが数としてしか見えなくなる。数量です。遡れば第一次大戦だと思いますが。二十世紀の戦争が、身体を物量化する、数量化する、データ化するという、変換の技術を見いだし、その結実として、いまや数えることさえできなくなったイラク兵の砂漠のなかの死体があるんだ、まさに「亡き骸」としてある、というふうに私には思えたんです。

鴻　実際には見ていないわけですから、それは、想像力のなかでの無数の死体ですよね。そういうふうな場所に置かれている死体の状況、あるいは人間の状況と言い換えていいと思うんだけど、それを現実化していく。

清水　ええ。舞台化する。

鴻　舞台化していくときに、実際には役者が出てくるわけだから、肉体が登場してくる。その意味で言うと、舞台に現れてくる肉体というのは、イラク兵の無数の死体を背負って、

清水　いや、それは不可能ですよね。それは表象不可能です。ですから、当時、表象の問題を根底的に考えざるをえなかったというこ
となんですが、単にこの事件について説明するとか、別の何かに置き換えて代行させるとかそういうことではない。それでは隠されている身体は現れてこない。私が考えたのは、ある行為のただなかに、つまり行為を遂行している、その最中に、特異な出来事が反復してくるのではないかと。

鴻　形態的に反復するということ？

清水　というか、むしろ形が初めにあるわけです。多分に渾沌とはしていますが……。一例ですが、たとえば私はある特定の写真、映画、絵画、テクストなどについて役者と話します。そこから形を創っていく。しかしこのままではまだ日常の、単なるジェスチュアにすぎない。どんなに言葉を注ぎ込んでもだめです。表象になるためには決定的な出来事がいる。

鴻　イラクで起こったことが？

清水　いや、そうではなくて。

鴻　どの出来事ですか？

拘束系と身体の逸脱

清水　わかりやすい例で言うと、我々の「動き」の稽古で拘束系というのがある。文字通り、上半身をこうグッと押さえつけられる、拘束されるわけです。拘束される、離れる。また拘束される、また離れる。これを繰り返し稽古していたときに、ある一人の女優の身体が、異様な逸脱の仕方をしはじめたわけです。それは必ずそのシーンで起こる。特定の拘束系のシーンにおける彼女に限って起こる。稽古のあとで訊いてみたら、「私の最初の記憶は、母から文字を習ったということ。これ右手を添えられて手習いよね。けれど、どうしても書けなかった文字が『ま』っていう字だったの。すると母は怒って『ママのまの字だから絶対に書きなさい。許さない』と言って私のからだを押さえつけて……」
そんなふうに、たとえば三十年前に封印し

たはずの記憶がいまこの「動き」のなかで「反復」される。このような事態として表象というものが捉えられないか。イラク兵の死体の表象が不可能な以上、演技における「反復」の表象不可能性というもので拮抗できないか。そういう方法をとりはじめたように思います。

鴻　ということは、少なくとも、イラクで起こったことを表象するということとはしていないわけですか？

清水　そうですね。

鴻　でも、それについて考えてはいるわけですね？

清水　そうですね。不可能です。

鴻　そもそも考えてなければ出てこない。

清水　つまり、考えてはいるが、再現的な表象は不能だから、再現はしていない。問題は、それに拮抗する表象の形式、それは表象でもないわけか。表象の不可能性としての行為を具体化していくときに、表象の問題が現れる。

清水　その事が、まさにいま世界で起こっている出来事と反響し合わなければならない。

鴻　つまり、表象不可能性と関わる関わり方において、イラクにおける表象不可能性と関

わるということですね？

清水　ええ。

鴻　結局、そういう試みをするためには、無数に展開されているそうした表象不可能な世界における出来事と関係をとっていかなければ、どうにもならない。

表象不可能をどう表象するか

清水　繰り返しますが、それこそ想像力の問題です。何が起こっているのか、何が隠されたのか、どのような身体性が監禁されているのか、常に政治的な想像力を働かせていないといけない。心構えを言えば、何か自分だけは何に反応すべきなのかが問題になる。超越的なポジションにいて、理論やメソッドを構築したからこれで明日もやっていけるなどという時代ではないですよ。とくに外国をツアーするときは状況と密接に絡みながら、その都度、その場で、作品構成を組み替えていかないと、ある一定のこの作品がどうのっていうようなことではまったくないんです。作品の普遍性などはもはやない。たとえば、数年前のクロアチアでの体験ですが、走っている普通の自家用車のトランクから機関銃が飛び出しているような場所で表象不可能性をどう表象するか。紋切型に落ちない。難民がすぐ郊外の山にいるところでは、とくにそのぎりぎりのところで突破していかないと拮抗できない。

グローバリゼーションが露出させるもの

鴻　そうなってくると、日本においてそれをやろうというときに、日本にはいわゆるザグレブ的な難民がいるわけではないので、我々は何に反応すべきなのかが問題になる。先程グローバリゼーションという言葉によって隠蔽されてくるものもあるということを言っていたけれど、逆にグローバリゼーションによって露出してくるものもないわけではない。さまざまな問題は、多様な形で露出してきたり、隠蔽されたりしているわけです。グローバリゼーションというと均質化が問題にされることが多いが、逆に、そのことによって差異性が露出してくることもある。それにアーティストは答えなければならない。たとえば、シカゴ大学のアリウン・アパドゥライは、グローバリゼーションとシティ・カルチャーとの関係を問題にしていて、そこからトイレット問題という争点を抽出してきたりする。つまり、グローバリゼーションがボンベイという街で問題化させたのは、衛生システムとトイレット問題だというんです。ボンベイのスラムにおいて、トイレット問題は昔からあったにちがいないのだが、グローバリゼーションのなかで緊急な課題として浮上してくる。それはほとんど解決不能だけれど、だけど一つずつトイレットをつくっていくプロジェクトができてくるわけです。途方もなく先に、もしかしたら解決するかもしれないけれど、スラムにおいては半ば解決不可能な問題として提示されているわけです。そこで何が問われるのかというと、日本のホームレスにはトイレット問題はないですよね。要するに、公園に住んでいるから、公衆便所がある。あるいは、ホームレスの問題はもちろん問題です

が、日本における主要な問題かどうかはよくわからないわけです。いや、もっと難解で深刻な問題があるにちがいないのです。それが何なのかがはっきりしない。たとえばザグレブの郊外における難民問題というのは、ある種、露出している問題だと思います。清水さんたちが、それに応答しようとしてザグレブで上演する。それが簡単だとは言いませんが、日本で上演するときには、いったい何に応答しようとするのか。何が問題として存在しているのか。つまり、それこそ表象不可能なものとして、存在するかもしれない日本文化における問題性のどこと接続するのか。「闘争としての身体」は何と切り結んでいるのかということですよね。

清水　端的に、それは身体に課せられている暴力ですね。私の舞台構成の手法とクロスさせて言えば、まず身体を攻囲している視線の暴力を露呈させる。権力の構造が明るみに出るや否やメディア・イメージがすぐさまこの構造を脱構築する。身体は隠され、構造は中吊りのまま存続する。反動言説が分析、洗脳、調教を行う。

鴻　具体的に言うと？

ドメスティック・バイオレンスの起源

清水　たとえば私の演出に特徴的な暴力シーンですが、いまや日本の観客のほとんどはこれをドメスティック・バイオレンスだと見なしています。虐待であると。私は、この変化を進歩だと思いたい。数年前はそうではなかった。叩かれている女優の背中が赤く充血していくとき、それが天使の翼のようだとか、殴るリズムに生命の鼓動を感じるとか（笑）。けれど一方で、この暴力をひたすら諸個人の人間性の問題に解消していこうとする勢力がある。原因は「心の闇」であると。「心の闇」なんて誰にもわかるわけないですよ。文字通り「闇」なんですから（笑）。この暴力はかつての暴力――夫婦げんかや厳格な躾などとは違うのであれば、なぜこうも生み出されているのか。すなわちドメスティック・バイオレンスを生み出している構造自体を（上演において）問い、批判していくことこそ、演劇のなすべきことであるはずです。

鴻　もっとはっきり言ってしまえば、グローバリゼーションの所産だということですよね。温床は国家・資本主義です。

清水　そうです。一方では家族（血縁共同体）の解体を促しながら、他方では家族（税収の対象）に寄生する。こんな空虚なカラクリはみんな知っているんです。「闇」のなかにあるような事柄ではまったくない。

鴻　そうすると、いわゆるグローバリゼーションという事態にどう応答するか、あるいはどう反逆するかという問題が非常に重要な問題であるわけです。ある意味で言うと、いまグローバリゼーション流行りだけれども、演劇に限らず、現代のアーティストは、グローバリゼーションとどう闘うかという問題を抱えているわけですよね。たとえば、日本の場合だと、グローバリゼーションのなかで何が起こっているかというと、いわゆるナショナリズムの台頭、つまり外部性の排除で

清水　そうです。陰湿なレイシズム。

鴻　もしかしたら、差異化し、分裂し、異質化していく可能性をも孕んでいるかもしれないグローバリゼーションという動きに対して、資本主義のなかでの現実の動きは、可能性の部分を次々に剥奪していくことによって、ある地域をできるだけ均一の形に押し込める民族主義的な方法へ乖離させていくという、ある意味ではそれと矛盾した動きをしようとしている。そのことによって、権力はより強く身体を管理しなくてはいけなくなるという構造が起こっているわけですよね。

清水　ほんとに脅迫的なガイドライン・キャンペーンですよ。「もっと監視を！　もっと規律を！」とか、自警団にでもなったようなつもりで掛け声かけて。

鴻　そういうようなところで、日本の演劇が保守化しているわけだ。

清水　よくいわれているように、いまグローバリゼーションに対抗するものは「トランス・ナショナリズム」と言えば新しそうだが、つまるところこれはかつての帝国主義ですよね。もう一つは原理主義。ありていに言えば、日本はこのどちらも選べないというので、ナショナリズムが跋扈しはじめてるわけですよ。

しかし昨今の審美主義への回帰みたいなもので成立している日本の芸術作品は、まあ諸外国から一定の評価を受けている他ジャンルのものなら別ですが、演劇はちょっとその方向は無理なのではないかと思います。率直に言って、いまの世界の演劇マーケットから見ても、つまりこのグローバリゼーションのただなかにおいて進行しているアート・ツーリズムの枠組みのなかで見ても、そこはまさに表現の強度、思考の水準を革新すべく、新たなアーティストたちが凌ぎを削ってサバイブしているわけで、しかもこれらは皆、多文化主義で動いている。そのような状況で、日本の、それも復古主義的ないわゆる「ナショナリスティック・アート」がなんらかの評価を受けるとはまず考えにくい。

鴻　それはたぶん無理なのかもしれないけれども、試みとしてあるんじゃないかという問題はあるわけです。

清水　嫌ですね。相手にされないだけですよ。

拓本文化的エンターテインメントと日本

鴻　九〇年代以降の日本の演劇の全体的な流れのなかで、清水さんは孤立しているわけですが、どうして孤立しているかというと、グローバリゼーションのただなかで、日本においては国民の演劇を創生するという大きなプロジェクトが展開されているからです。現代演劇のための新国立劇場が一九九七年にオープンしたことも、単に喜んでいられない出来事なのであって、その動きに向けて、九〇年代に大きな流れがあったわけですが、この劇場を中心に、日本の現代演劇はものすごく国民主義的な、ドメスティックな価値観をもとに展開しはじめたんです。それが九七年に実に展開しはじめたわけです。それが九七年に実現するということ自体が、九〇年代の演劇の展開を象徴しているわけです。それと、演劇自体も外部とのリンクをほとんど持たない。戦争がモチーフになっている演劇などが作ら

れても、加藤典洋の「敗戦後論」が、国内問題として、戦争責任やその倫理の問題を語るように、戦争の問題が実にドメスティックに演劇化される。たとえば、フィリピンの捕虜収容所を舞台にしたような作品を鐘下辰男が書く。それは『ビルマの竪琴』と同じですが、そこには日本人しか出てこない。こうした感覚が可能になるくらいに、グローバリゼーションのなかで世界との交信に可能性があったような状況はまったく無化されてしまうんです。ほとんどすべての作品はその方向で動いてますよね。日本の現実とリンクするような形での表象を提示しているような演劇があるとすれば、それはむしろどちらかというと、風俗的な現象にコミットしているようなものです。そういうのを「拓本文化」と言うらしいけど。

清水　タクホンというのは？

鴻　拓本というのは、墓石の表面に紙を置いて、ポンポンとたたくと、字が浮かび上がってくるもので、現実に深くコミットし分

悲劇の逆説と崇高性

演劇というのは現実に対する応答です。現実に対する応答というのは、たとえばギリシャ演劇がまさにそうで、神々の神託の通り

析しているのではなくて、拓本的に写し取っているということです。少なくともその演劇を観れば、たとえばケラリーノ・サンドロヴィッチの「ナイロン100℃」とかがやっている演劇は、拓本文化的エンターティンメントなんです。だから、そこへ行くと、もしかしたらそういうような女の子がいるかなという女の子が出てきたり、もしかしたら、そういう家庭があるかなというような現代の家庭が描かれていたりする。でも、それは一応エンターティンメントの系列のなかに、いわば写し変えられた一つの現実、拓本性というようなもので、私は、そこから演劇が活性化するある。あるいは我々に何かを考えさせるというものが出てくるようには思えないわけですが。

に滅びていくオイディプスのことが上演されますよね。オイディプスの悲劇というのは、神々の神託の通りにオイディプスが生きてしまうことです。でも、ヴァルター・ベンヤミン（一八九二─一九四〇）の『ドイツ悲劇の根源』に依拠すれば、そこに人間の敗北だけを見るのは誤りなのです。つまり、実際には神々に敗北するオイディプスが描かれているのに、非常に奇妙なことに、あのオイディプスを見ているギリシャの人たちは、それを見ることによって神々の企みを拒絶するわけです。その決断こそが重要なわけです。つまり、神々を拒絶する場所として、ギリシャ悲劇がある。神々の秩序というのは、それまでギリシャ人を支配していた秩序です。その秩序の中で滅びていく人間を描くことによって、彼らは神々の秩序を拒絶しているわけです。その神々の秩序を拒絶する人間の登場にこそギリシャ演劇の逆説的な人間の姿、その非力な人間が圧倒的な優位に立っている神々を拒絶する瞬間こそ、神々の没落が始まったときなのです。私は、このような悲劇の出現の構造のなかに、

演劇の可能性があると思っている。表象不可能という問題もそこに関連してくると思う。つまり、日本の現実のなかで、それを描くときにその意識があるかどうかということが問題なのです。私がつい最近観た演劇のなかで、かなり感動したというか、驚きをもって七時間を過ごした芝居があるのですが、それはそうした表象不可能性と決断に関わる演劇でした。ベルギーのグループオフというのがルワンダの人たちと作った、「ルワンダ'94」という虐殺に関わる演劇です。

表象の限界と証言の演劇

ベルギーはルワンダを支配していた国ですけど、ベルギーが撤退した後、民族抗争が再燃します。それが一つの原因となって、虐殺が始まり、その虐殺のなかを生き延びた人がいるわけです。その生き延びた人たちの一人が、この劇の冒頭で、自分が目撃したことを証言する。これは目撃したことを証言するのであって、その問題をどう解決したらいいかということを我々に伝えているものではないんです。そして、さらにこの集団の人たちはルワンダに行ったりしながら、さまざまな証言を集め、事実関係を一生懸命調べてくる。そうすると、いろいろな素材、ドキュメントが出てくる。実際に、虐殺の光景を隠し撮りでカメラに収められていたりして、そういう映像を流すわけです。我々はそれを観る。さらに、死者たちの証言のようにさまざまなテキストが我々に提示されてくる。「そういうものを公にするのはやめた方がいいんじゃないか」と言う人がいるなかで、ドラマの構造としては、BBBというニュースキャスターが「いや、我々はそれを見なくちゃいけないんだ」と言いながら、事実を明らかにしようという運動を現実化していく。劇の展開として、我々はその推移を見たり聞いたりする。結局、そこで何が起こっているかというと、防げなかった虐殺の事実がより詳細に我々に伝えられてくるわけです。それを防ぐ方法は何も提示されていないんですが、問題はそこで我々が何を考えるかということです。つまり、圧倒的な非力のなかで、それを拒絶するという決断をそこでするわけです。演劇というのは、そうした決断の場として存在しうる。でも、それは誰かの証言とともに行われる。生き延びた者たちが、死者たちの声を彼らに代わって語る。それは歴史を構築する作業以外の何ものでもない。証言と歴史の構築、そして、現実に起きたことに対する根底的否認、そうしたことこそが演劇という空間においてなされているのだということを、最初に発見したのはギリシャ人だと思います。そして、二十世紀の重要な演劇人たちが我々に伝えてきたのも、実は、そうした演劇の力でした。タデウシュ・カントールなどはまさにそういう演劇を作っていたわけです。

だから、そういう意味で言うと、先程の表象不可能性ということから問題が始まっているわけですが、でも、その表象不可能性へ演劇の形式は接近しようとするものなのです。表象不可能なものと関わろうとする形式として「証言」というものがあり、それを契機として二十世紀の重要な演劇は成立している。カン

トール自身、「死者たちは証言する」という言い方を何度もしていますが、現代劇の可能性の一つとして、私はいま証言によって過去を歴史化していく場としての演劇というものを考えている。そして、先程からの話を聞いていると、清水さんもそういうことを行うのが演劇であると考えて、演劇と関わっているのではないかと私には見えるわけです。

清水　はい。そうあらねばと。

鴻　私はいま、来年、ハンブルグで開催されるラオコオン・フェスティバル二〇〇二の構想を練っているのですが、その統一テーマを「ヒストリー&メモリー」としたらどうだろうかと考えています。awakening（覚醒すること）というベンヤミンの概念が軸になります。カントールは「終わりが近づいてくるものがある」と言いました。しかし、我々は二〇〇〇年という時を通過して、二〇〇一年にいるわけです。我々は新たな方法が必要です。だから、我々の意識を少し変える必要があると思う。我々は二十世紀から二十一世紀に向けて目覚めつつある。ならば、覚醒していく最初の瞬間に何を我々は想起するのか。目覚めの瞬間に我々が記憶している夢はすぐに忘却されるだろう。ならば、それを忘却する前に、いかにして分析し、定着させていくべきなのか。この作業こそが歴史という作業ではないのか。おそらく、それが現代演劇を考えるときに非常に重要なモチーフになってくると私は思っているんです。

なぜなら、「いま・ここ」で上演される演劇という形式は、まさに過去を現在時において批判的に再配置する方法でもあるからです。先程、清水さんが言っていた身体ですが、「ま」という字が書けないとか、そういうある作業から出てきた事態は、生き延びた者の証言ということに繋がりがあるのではないかと思うのです。

告白の陥穽

清水　ええ、そうなんですが、繋げるために新たな方法が必要です。そうでないと、我々がそのまま舞台で表現しても単なる告白に終わってしまうんです。その告白をどうしたら証言に繋げられるかという、まさにこの「どうしたら」が問われている。これはこのあとの作品分析で具体的な議論になると思いますが、いまここで言えることは、告白から証言に向かうべき回路が一見、閉ざされているかのように見えるのは、まさに「身体」が奪われているからです。唯一それを語ることができるはずの彼・彼女の「身体」が、メディア・イメージによってすでに強奪されている。たとえば先程、ルワンダの話がありましたが、私は衛星放送で見ました。

鴻　ルワンダの事件そのものですか？

清水　そのものというか、なぜ虐殺が起こったのかを関係者たちの証言によって検証しているものです。たしか九七年だったと思います。「零カテゴリー」という舞台で音声を一部使用したこともあって、よく覚えているのですが。

鴻　芝居ではなくて？

清水　ええ、芝居ではなくて。「ルワンダの悲劇」というカナダのアルターシネが制作した

ドキュメンタリーなんですが……私が最も驚愕したのは、ある監獄の光景でした。とにかく膨大な人々が囚われている。狭い獄で身を横たえることができない。ずっと突っ立ったままで、排泄も自分の足下に垂れ流すほかない。足の傷が腐ってきて壊疽になる。多くの人たちがその壊疽になった足を切り落とされて、その場に崩れ落ちている。そこにテレビカメラが向けられる。むろんみな一言もない。すると、一人の男が腐りかけている自分の足の親指を引きちぎってカメラに向けて投げたと、番組では紹介していました。また最近、ボスニアにおける虐殺のドキュメントも放映されましたね。当時、国連軍の中枢にいた現場のオランダ軍将校の証言とか、いろいろ事細かに出てくるわけです。その将校は、自分たちがここで難民たちを見捨てて撤退してしまったら、間違いなくこの難民たちはここで虐殺されるということがわかっていながら、撤退して本国に帰ってしまうんです。そういう人の証言は苦渋に満ちていて、「あのとき…」みたいな感じでまるで、俳優のように語りだ

す。それは告白だと思うんですよ。告白ではなくて、本当に証言すべき当事者たちの、犠牲者たちの声は、ただの一言もないんです。みな呆然といつもただ突っ立っている。ボスニアの方はまだ幾分か声はありました。けれどルワンダとなると、こういう映像ばかりで、とにかく一言もないんです。私は本当に、「何か言ってくれ！」というふうに叫びたくなるのですが、ただただいつも突っ立っているだけの映像なんです。この事態をたとえば、「屠殺される寸前の家畜のように」などと言ったり書いたりしてしまえば了解はされるだろうが、決して「表象」には届かないでしょう。これらの身体は、「詩」なんかではないんです。文学ではないんです。鴻さんの言葉を借りるなら、圧倒的に非力なまま、立ち尽くしたままの、まさにこの「身体それ自体」がそのまま証言だと思います。証言というのは、それは言説として、言葉として説明されなくとも、身体に差し向けられた眼差しのなかで、あるいはまた「反復」という事態を汲み取ろうとする想像力を通して、証言というものをすくい出すことができる。私としては、そのような手法をもっともっと開拓したいと、せつに思うんです。

零カテゴリー＠東京芸術劇場（1997）

第二部

鴻　これまで我々は、作家が作品を作ってい

くときに、どういうふうに世界を見ているか、それと表現をどう繋げるかなど、やや原則論的な話をしてきたわけですが、そろそろ九〇年代の解体社の活動に具体的に触れていきたいと思います。身体における帝国主義とか、資本主義的な抑圧の形式とかが、八〇年代の「イメージの演劇」の本質だったのではないかと言っていましたが、それは非常に重要な問題ですけど、その後、実際に作品自身が変わっていくわけですよね。その変化というのは、自分の作品を自分で分析すると、どういうふうなところにあると考えていますか。

清水　そうですね、上演に即してお話しすると、『THE DOG』と『TOKYO GHETTO』ですか。犬（THE DOG）の方は、先程お話したように、二年の空白を経て新たなメンバーとともに本郷にアトリエをつくったときの旗揚げ公演ですね。九三年です。その年、アメリカに行っています。当時、イメージの演劇をどのように切断するか、できるかということ

演技、暴力、挑発

鴻　何が挑発的だったのですか？

清水　身体に対して直接的に行使される暴力です。実際に、男性が女性の背中を、彼の体力の限界まで、叩く。二十分ほど叩き続ける。

鴻　他人の体を叩くという形で行使される暴力。

清水　まずもってこれは違反なんですよ。ヨーロッパの舞台表現において、暴力は暗示させるだけの、それこそ単に表象です。

鴻　舞台で実際には叩かない。

かり考えていました。それと身体の政治性についてです。九五年に初演した『TOKYO GHETTO』は、ヨーロッパ、韓国をツアーしています。暴力に晒された身体の表象がテーマでした。方法的には、解体あるいは内破という演出に、より意識的になったともするのは、言ってみればタブーです。私としては、この作品がなぜあれほどまでにあの時期ヨーロッパの観客を挑発したか、いま総括してみたい。

鴻　普通、通俗的に言ってしまえば、殴る（頬を叩く）シーンというのは、自分の手のひらを叩くわけですよね。そういうふうにして、殴られたとするのが映画でも演劇でもよくあるわけだけど、実際に叩く・殴る。

清水　ええ。私が示したかったのは、先程の証言の話に関連させて言えば、いわばノンフィクショナリズムの可能性と言えるようなものです。まぎれもない事実と、行為をし続けることの限界、すなわち叩いているという事実、叩き続けるという行為、それだけで事実と行為だけで構成された舞台を目指した。とくに演出にとって重要なことは、観客に対し、この行為に何の説明も与えないことでした。これこんなわけで殴っているんです

清水　舞台では、通常、暴力は暗示・表象されるだけです。性行為を行う舞台や自分のからだを切り刻んだりするパフォーマンスは見たことがありますが、このような暴力、つまり舞台上の身体が、しかも他人から、相当なダメージを受けるような暴力そのものを提示

よといった、理由づけや動機、要因をいっさい示さない。劇場が新鮮な不安に満たされるまで、因果も善悪も決定不能のまま放置する。
…？

清水　いま思えば、私のこうした演出というものに対する構え自体が、あれほど挑発した理由かもしれない。いずれにしても暴力と不安は、いまもってグローバルな演劇表象として、ポジティブに機能しうる、対話ができる、ということをこのツアーが教えてくれた。

もう一つは、端的にオリエンタリズムがあった。

鴻　アジア。

清水　東洋ですね。私は東西の境界はとうにないと思っていた。

鴻　彼らにはあるけれど、私にはない。

東西から南北へ‥

清水　ええ、私は南と北の境界を提示していた。

鴻　ちょっとわかりにくいので、もう少し詳しく訊きます。つまり、身体というのがいわば制度化された存在であるし、しかもそれをどう操

るかということをめぐる、さまざまな技法みたいなものを考えていくという意味で言えば…す。

たしか、アルトーは、「人間の身体はうまくつくられていない、秩序も調和もなにもない」というふうなことを書いています。土方も「生まれてきたことが即興である」と発言してる。

清水　「動き」ですね。

鴻　動きを考えていくと、能や歌舞伎の身体も、舞踏の身体も、同じではないかもしれないけれど、そういう舞台上、役者としての身体を考えたことが制度である」と言っている。私にはそう聞こえる。アドルノが言うように、疑いもない、く私は『啓蒙の時代』を生きています。けれども私の、いまのこの身体は、いつだってその結果を、すなわち『啓蒙の結果』を生かされているにすぎない。ですから私という人間のこの身体の自由を目指すならば、この身体の様態を人間以外の生き物に徹底した加工をほどこす、その動きに徹底した加工をほどこす、当然のことです。あたりまえのようにみなやってきたことです。

清水　たとえば、世阿弥の「花」、アルトーの「分身」、土方巽の「剥製」、バリのケチャ、インドのカタカリ、クラシック（バレエ）、マーサ・グラハムの「コントラクション」、コンタクト・インプロビゼーション、フォーサイスの「置き去りにされた身体」であれ、根本はみなたった一つのことに関わっている。言い換えれば、禁止なしの「動き」は可能か、という絶対的な事柄にで

鴻　別に能・歌舞伎だからではない、ということを言っているんですね。能・歌舞伎でなくても、マーサ・グラハムでもそうである、クラシックでもそうであると。すべからく身体表象というのは、みんなそうである。だから、そ

清水　いや、同じですよ。みな同じことを言っている。

鴻　だから、それとは違わないわけですね、いま言っている話というのは？

16

111

う言うと、東西という考え方に問題があると。

清水　そもそもこの境界は、地政学的にはとう
に消え去っているわけですよ。冷戦の時代から、
米ソの宇宙戦略があったわけですから。ただ具
体的な身体がふれあう演劇のような文化実践の
現場では、むしろ個々のアイデンティティーを
保証するラインとして、いまだ強固に認識され
ています。それはヨーロッパばかりでなく、昨
年のこの香港公演でも感じたことです。ともかく、
このような「安定化」に向かう回復願望は、そ
れこそ拒絶していかねばならない。

鴻　なるほど。その東西という考え方が無効化
されたなかで、出現してくるのは南北の問題と
いうことですか?

清水　階級分化です。階級分裂ということ。

鴻　南北問題と身体の関係をもう少し語っても
らえますか。

アジア的身体という神話

清水　ですから、まさにそれは「反復」とル
ワンダ難民の表象不可能性をどう繋げるかと

いう方法意識と、告白と証言とを繋げていく
手法の政治性、歴史性にかかっている。

二、三、思い出話をさせてもらえば、九五
年の「TOKYO GHETTO」の初演のとき、
鴻さんが、女優たちの身体を評して「従軍慰
安婦だ」と言われたのを覚えています。私は
勇気づけられました。だって彼女たちは、数
十分の間、ただ丸椅子に座って押し黙ってい
るだけだったんです。また、このころ外国の
プロデューサーたちが少なからず私たちの稽
古場を訪れるようになりましたが、あまりよ
い反応ではなかった。「私が見たいのはアジア
的優しさなんだ」などと言う人もいましたね。
アジアにだって南京虐殺もあったし、サハ
コーもあった。無視されては困る。忘れては
いけないですよ。アーティストには責任があ
るんです、いまだにこれらを生み出す構造を
放置している責任が。私の舞台は、ますます
寡黙になって、以前より身体を晒していくよ
うになった。裸体をあつかうようになった。
汗、重さ、皮膚、血、涙といった、一度は捨
てたはずの身体の物質性が再び稽古場に回帰

してきた。これらをどのように歴史と接続さ
せていくか。

もう一つは、またも「イメージの演劇」で
す。先程グローバリゼーションに対抗するも
のとして、トランス・ナショナリズムという
ことを言いましたが、イメージの演劇の可能
性を考えはじめました。ひどく矛盾している
ようですが……。

鴻　それも有効であると。

清水　なぜかトランス・ナショナリズムな
んですよ。ビジョンにおいて。

鴻　清水さんにとって、トランス・ナショナ
リズムはイメージなんだ。

清水　ある閉じられた空間の内部で、それぞ
れの身体がそれぞれの形でもって多種多様に
自己実現するための井戸を掘る。いや掘って
いるかのように見せている。けれど実際は、
身体は構成体のパーツにすぎない。初めの方
で指摘しましたが、ここでの身体は、あくま
で媒体でありオブジェなんです。最初の方の
議論に戻ると、そこで意図的に消し去られて
いるのが、権力、強制力なんです。とくに、

いま流通しているイメージの演劇の構造は、おおむね、それが誰彼の強制力なしに行われているかのように、つまりそれぞれの身体が自律して、あたかも自発的に動いているかのような世界を観客にイメージさせている。これは簡単に批判できないですよ。「平和」が目指されているんですから。権力関係、政治性を消去しながら。自律や平和を悪く言う人はいない。したがって世界化する。「平和」を目指しているから戦争が起こるのだと、私はイメージの演劇に対して言いたいわけです。

ボーダレスと内破の手法

鴻　そういう意味で言うと、イメージの演劇というのは、舞台表象の普遍性の神話と繋がるわけです。つまり、演劇は世界に通用する。演劇は普遍的だという、要するに、日本人だけにわかるものではなくて、この優れた演劇、舞台は、アメリカ人にもわかるし、アフリカに行っても高く評価されるはずだという普遍の神話があって、それと非常に密接に関わるような形で、イメージの演劇というのが出現してくる。だから、イメージの演劇というのは、どちらかというと、普通の演劇の記述言語としての言語性は少ない。イメージ言語はあるかもしれないけど。

そのようなこともあって、一見みんなにわかるものとして流通したため、演劇よりもダンスの方がいいのではないかということも含めて、世界性を持ちうるのではないかということを言ってしまうような、ボーダレスということが非常に脳天気に語られるようなときに、イメージの演劇が世界に流通するということでもあったわけです。実は、それ自体が批判されていかなければならなかったということに、九〇年代に入って、何人かの人が気づき始めていったということですね。

清水　ええ、私の方法はどうしようもなく「解体」ですから、これを批判するには、構造のなかに入っちゃって、これを批判するというふうに内側から機能不全にしていく、内破していくという手法をとっていたんですが、それだけでは充分でない、何かいる、すなわち「切断」がいると。以前、私は「切断」というのは、光やオブジェ、音、映像などの諸要素が、鋭く空間を切断しているとか、いわゆるセノグラフィの構築のことだと勘違いしていた。そうではなく「意味」なんですね。イメージの演劇を切断するのは「意味」です。言語と言ってもいい。当時、私が意味として持っていたのは憲法九条とジェンダーです。これらを一定の持続、イメージの持続の限界地点で「切断」のために使った。

エイズの身体

鴻　八〇年代のアメリカを例にとると、八八〜八九年から演劇が政治化するわけですけど、要するに表象のポリティクスということがいわれて、実際に現実的・文化的な争点とどういうふうに呼応しているのか、表現者にとって非常に重要な問題になってきて、実際に舞台に出てくる人たちもその問題と関わるわけです。たとえば身体というのは、実際にエイズとかそういう問題と関わりつつ、先程、

内破と言っていたけど、内側から崩壊していく。そのような人が近くにいたり、あるいは都市のなかで増えてくるとかで、あるいは本人たちが実際にそうであるとかで、身体に向ける眼差しが変わるわけですよね。

一九六三─一九九五）は、「初めてエイズであると認識したときに、最初にしたことは自分の便を見たことだ」と言っていますが、その便を見たことで、いままでとは違った形で自分の便を見つめるようになる。便というのは、自分のからだの中から出てきて外側に行く、いわば自分であると同時に、自分でないようなものであるわけだけど、その形態、色、あるいは水分の状態をじっと見るようになった。それによって若干ずれても別に何の問題もないと思うんですが。

九五年に死んでしまったレザ・アブドー

だから、そういう形で存在してきた人間の肉体的・身体的状況が、彼が演劇を作るときの非常に重要な契機になっている。そのなかから、晒されている身体が彼の演劇に極めて重要に撮られている。それは一九八八～一九八九年から現れる形式の内部において、八〇年代の終わりぐらいから内側から壊れていったわけです。それに気づくか、あるいはそこに関わるかどうかの大きな問題がある。いつ気づくかは、人によって若干ずれても別に何の問題もないと思うに思える。そういった問題を含めて、たとえば九三、九四年に自覚されはじめた問題というのは、ここ数年のなかで、どういうふうなところに立ち至っているのでしょうか？

九〇年代に向けての人間の置かれている状況と演劇が非常に密接に関わり、そして、人間の置かれている状況こそが演劇であるという事態が起こってきているのです。そういう意味で言うと、イメージの演劇自体が、実は演劇という表現の変動──世界自体がある危機的な状況に向けて動いていくときに、多くの演出家たちによって目撃され感じられたことだったと思うんです。それを清水さんは湾岸戦争を契機に掴んだ。アブドーは九五年に死んでしまったけれど、事態は変わっているように思える。そういった問題を含めて、たとえば九三、九四年に自覚されはじめた問題というのは、ここ数年のなかで、どういうふうなところに立ち至っているのでしょうか？

清水 プロセニアムですか？

鴻 工場みたいなところでやる。それを写真に撮ると、まったく同じではないんだけど、それこそイメージの演劇が意味で切断されている印象を受ける。それが、おそらく八〇年代から九〇年代への移行期のなかで世界の現実の変動──世界自体がある危機的な状況へ向けて動いていくときに、多くの演出家たちによって目撃され感じられたことだったと思う

清水 やはり話しておきたいのは、クロアチ

劇場空間における分断線

まり、非常に大きな舞台で造形的に作品が作られていく。

そういうなかで、いま清水さんは「意味で切断する」と言ったわけですが、それはまさにアブドーにおいてもそうで、アブドーの演劇もイメージの演劇みたいなんですよね。非常にスペクタクラーで、ロバート・ウィルソン（一九四一─）の次の世代だといわれたりもする。つ

アのザグレブで「TOKYO GHETTO」を上演したときのことですが、上演中、観客に乱入されて二度ほど舞台が中断したことがあるんです。私は、その事態を、たとえば舞台と客席がそこで境界を消失したとか、消失して何か融合してしたとか、そんなことではまったくないのだと考えています。この切迫した一瞬の中断がとても重要なんだと思うんです。その一瞬がいってもわずか数秒なんですが、その、いま、分断線が引かれているのだと感じた。

男優が女優を叩いているわけです。そこに一人の観客（男性）が客席からザーッとやってきて、叩いている男優の足をバッとすくった。「やめろ！」と。そうしたら男優がバーンとひっくり返って、それで場内は大喝采です。そのとき彼は男優に「何だこの野郎！」と見返されると思ったんですね。だけど、男優は振り返らずに、また叩きはじめたんです。「Stop it」と口々に叫びはじめた。そのなか

を彼は再び英雄のようにやってきて、また男優は足をすくわれひっくり返ったのですが、むろん見返すこともなくまた叩きはじめたんです。もし三回目が始まったら、もうほとんど収拾がつかないので、私も舞台に上がって「とにかく最後まで見てくれ」と言おうと思っていたところ、三回目の前でシーンがパッと変わり、そのまま上演は続けることができました。

何が言いたいのかというと、彼は見返されることを期待して、二回来たんだと思います。つまるところ、彼のなかで、自分が想像だにしていない、他なるもの、自分とは決定的に異なる他者に、つまり他の身体性に遭遇したんです。そこで線が引かれたのではないかと、私は思っています。要するに、普段、隠されていて見ることのできない分断線が現れた。彼と男優の間に、分断線がシャーッと引かれた、ということです。その分断された身体性が、いわばイメージに監禁されていた身体性が、ふっと垣

間見える。意味として見える。

鴻　その観客にということですか？

清水　ええ。すべての観客に。

鴻　足を払った観客にも？

清水　おそらく、彼が最もよく見えたのです。彼は上演終了後にドイツの新聞記者からインタビューを受けて、「なぜ上演に介入したのか」という質問に対して、自分のしたこの行為について長々語っています。記事によれば、彼の住んでいるアパートの隣室の夫婦のことにふれています。「毎晩、夫が妻を殴っている。殴る音が聞こえてくる。自分はそれを止めたいのだが、夫は見るからに屈強で非力な自分はとてもかなわないそうにない。毎夜、妻の悲鳴を聞きながら、夫の殴る数を、ただ数えているだけだった。いままで自分は最低の人間であったけれども、今夜この劇場で、自分は、ついに止めることができたのだ」といった内容です。

鴻　何年のことですか？

清水　九六年です。ユーロカズ・フェスティバルという、次世代の先端的な舞台だけに焦

TOKYO GHETTO - Orgie @クロアチア・ザクレブ（1996）

点をあてて開催される国際演劇祭でのことで
す。私にとっては大事件だったこれを契機に、
「身体の演劇」についての理念に思いをめぐら
せました。イメージの演劇から「身体の演劇」
と言えばすんなりですが、そうではない。少
し厳密に言うと、まずイメージで、切断される。
味で、あるいはアクシデントで、切断される。

分断線が現れ、それによって、いままで監禁
され表象不可能だった「身体」が見える。ま
さにそのときに、イメージの演劇の切断面に、
人が共同体に帰還しないで、共同体の手前に
その切り取られた断面に「身体の演劇」が成
立する。

演劇と共同体からの離脱

鴻　それは、そのアクシデントによって、清
水さんが気づいたわけですよね。だけど、そ
ういうのが潜在的にあったわけですよね。そ
れまでは気づかなかったかもしれないけど、
分断線があるということが、そのことによっ
て意識されるようになったということですね。
いまの話を聞いていて私が思いだしたのは、
カントールがその分断線について書いていた
ことです。カントールにとって、演劇という
のは「死の演劇」なんですが、それは宗教
的・文化的共同性から離脱した者と関わって
いる。共同体から追放された者にはさまざま
な運命が待ち受けているわけだけれども、そ
の運命を背負いつつ、どこかに掻き消えてい

た人間が、こちらに戻ってくる。彼が共同体
に帰還してしまえば、普通の人だけど、その
人が共同体に帰還しないで、共同体の手前に
留まり、こちらに目を向けて佇んでいる。そ
れは異様な光景だが、そのような人間がそも
そも俳優の起源なのではないか、というのが
彼の考え方です。顔形は人間だけど、彼は
限りなく異質な存在なんです。「我々とはまつ
たく違う、まったく無縁の者が、見えざる越
えることの不可能な境界線の向こう側に佇ん
でこちらを見る瞬間こそが、我々が真に俳優
と出会うときであり、我々はそこに新たな人
間の誕生を予感して戦慄するのだ」とカン
トールは『死の演劇宣言』のなかで書いてい
ます。そのことが演劇の本質だと、彼は考え
ているわけです。そういうようなときに何が
起こるかというと、私は先程から観客論に話
をもっていこうとしているんだけど、このこ
とにおいても、観客が何かを発見するのであ
り、観客が新しい人間へと変貌する契機をそ
こで手にするわけです。そのためにこそ、向
こうは途方もなく異質なんです。それが演劇

の構造的本質です。カントールが「死の演劇」の理念として語ったことを、期せずして、いま清水さんは話しているわけです。日本の演劇評論家などを見ていても、基本的に共感の共同性が演劇であると思っている人が多いし、ギリシャ悲劇さえもそうだと思っている人が多い。ギリシャ演劇以来、演劇は客席と舞台とがいかに融合するかということを考えている、ギリシャの古代劇場が円形になって客席が舞台を取り囲んでいるのは、そういうことだと思っている人も多いですよね。

清水　実際、よくいわれてますね。

鴻　そして、たとえば近代劇場だと、舞台がちょっと高くなっていて、鰻の寝床のように客席があって、舞台と観客席が冷ややかだから、「その冷ややかさを取り除くために、野外の円形劇場を造りましょう」というふうに仮に誰かが言ったら、ほとんどの人が納得するわけでしょ。

清水　していますね。

鴻　（笑）でも、それはまったく演劇的でないということです。ぜんぜん演劇的でない話をしている。だから、いまみたいなアクシデントが派生することによって、明らかになってくることが、むしろ演劇的な出来事であり、演劇の本質的構造を改めて我々に知らせているということなんですよね。

最後に、清水さんがまさにいま考えていることを話してもらって終わりましょうか。

戦争身体、そして幻影姿態

清水　それは「戦争身体」です。これからの戦争によって生み出されるであろう身体と、かつての戦争によって見いだされた身体。前者は、先刻から話題にしている「身体の演劇」の流れで、その展開をさらに推し進めるものです。技法はフィジカル・ムーブメントですが、イメージとしては管理不全の「群れ」ですね。しかもこの「群れ」は光にあたると消えてしまう。いわばイラク兵の死体ですね。死の軍隊とよんでもいい。ともあれ、南北の階級をさらに分裂させてより多様な分断線を現出させたい。後者は、いままさに取り組んでいるニューロ・システム、あるいは幻影肢態（ファンタム・ペイン）とよんでいる技法ですが、いってみれば、寸断された身体知覚のバーチャル・アクチュアリティのことだと思ってもらえばいいと思います。

鴻　ない足が痛むみたいな。

清水　まさしく幻影です。引きちぎられた足の行方、失われた肢体の幻影を生きる身体、知覚だけで創られた「動き」、「気配」のシステムのなかで、この身体性がいかなるものかをはっきりと明示したい。いまは、この方法に賭けてますね。

鴻　なんでその問題が出てきたわけですか？

清水　九八年以降、メンバーがまた入れ替わりまして、若い彼・彼女らは俳優でもダンサーでもまったくない、そうしたものになる気もない、単に「身体」なんですね。こうした身体といつもゼロ地点から向き合える、ということは私にとってとても大事なんです。何が言いたいのかというと、一つは「身体の演劇」は絶えずイメージの演劇に回収されてしまう危機を、構造上、常に孕んでいます。

もし切断に失敗すれば観客の多くは安心してすぐさまそのイメージを消費するでしょう。綱渡りなんですよ。たとえば二、三年前から私の提示する身体がリアルであるといわれだした。リアルな身体などあるわけはない。結果を、制度を生きているんですから、前に言ったように、リアルはあるのではなく、「反復」として体験するのです。ですから本来、それは表象しえないものなんです。だからこのリアルはバーチャルに対抗して発明されたイメージ言語にすぎない、があそうであるがゆえに、あっというまに世界化する。しかし、そもそも私はそんなことをやっているのではない。私が汗、血、痛苦とか諸々のアブジェクションを舞台上に持ち出すのはリアルだからではないんです。バーチャルだから。重要なのはバーチャルの方です。まさにドット（点）と化した身体からどのように腕を、足を、肢体を知覚していくのか、加速するメディア・テクノロジーの進化のただなかで身体を攻囲する、監視・検索権力のアクチュアリティが緊急に問われているのです。

第二にその政治性です。私は当初、身体の歴史化です。結論から言えば、私はこの身体を「戦争身体」と接続させたい。第一次大戦後に初めて出現した身体、いわゆる塹壕身体ですね。前線の中の塹壕に何カ月も籠っていた兵士が、そこから逃げ出してきたときにフロイトによって見いだされたあの神経症です。今秋はおよそ三カ月にわたりヨーロッパ、アメリカに見いだされてくるわけですが、二十世紀初頭に見いだされた身体が、この二十一世紀の幕開けにおいて甦ってくる。そのような上演を通して、今後も世界の観客との対話を続けていきたい。

（おおとり　ひでなが／演劇批評家）

最後に歴史化です。つまりは「戦争身体」とに思えます。

クローン化のようなことを考えていました。クローン技術の進展は国家を無化してしまう。資本主義が国家に依存してきた労働者の生産を、国家なしでやれてしまうからです。身体ですね。資本主義みずから労働者を産めるのです。国家にとってそれはとうてい容認できるものではない。ですからグローバリゼーションにおいて、クローン人間の存在はいまのところ解決不可能な両義性を持っているわけです。先程、一新されたメンバーは単に身体だった、と言いましたが、私は彼・彼女らにクローン身体の表象の可能性を見ていたわけです。たとえば、生の緊張感をまったく失いながらも自分の身体を無機的な状態のまま持続させている、この身体は世界を見ることはない、ただ眼球の表面に映しだしているのみ。そのような鉱物質の身体性を通してクローンを表象できないか。この技法はまだ獲得できていませんが、作業は続けていきたい。いずれにせよ、自分のこの身体はすでに自分の所有物などではない、という認識がきわめて重要なこと

（しみず　しんじん／演出家）